Reclaiming the Body
in
Christian Spirituality

Reclaiming the Body
in
Christian Spirituality

edited by Thomas Ryan

Paulist Press
New York/Mahwah, N.J.

Unless otherwise noted, the scripture quotations outlined herein are from the New Revised Standard Version Bible with Apocrypha, copyright © 1989 by the Division of Christian Education of the National Council of Churches of Christ in the U.S.A. Used by permission.

Chapter 1 is a revised version of an article that originally appeared under the title of "The Body in Spiritual Practice" in *Spiritual Life* 47 (2001):200–15. It is reproduced with permission.

Cover design by Trudi Gershenov
Book design by Lynn Else

Library of Congress Cataloging-in-Publication Data

Reclaiming the body in Christian spirituality / edited by Thomas Ryan.
    p.   cm.
   Includes bibliographical references.
   ISBN 0-8091-4295-3 (alk paper)
   1. Body, Human—Religious aspects—Christianity. 2. Spiritual life—Christianity.
I. Ryan, Thomas, Father.

BT741.3.R43 2005
248—dc22

2004015169

Published by Paulist Press
997 Macarthur Boulevard
Mahwah, New Jersey 07430

www.paulistpress.com

Printed and bound in the
United States of America

Contents

Introduction

Why a book on reclaiming the body in Christian spirituality? What does the body need to be reclaimed from? Consider briefly the influence on us of those who have shaped our contemporary culture:

René Descartes (1596–1650) is generally regarded as the founder of modernity. In surveying the history of philosophical and religious thought, he despaired of finding any coherency, consistency, or certitude. He found the greatest minds—Plato, Aristotle, Cicero, Thomas Aquinas—at odds with each other. So Descartes decided to clear the decks and start afresh. In his *Discourse on Method*, he opines that if a proposition or conviction *can* be doubted, it *should* be doubted. He finds that the one thing he cannot doubt is that he is doubting. This becomes his starting point. He proceeds to found his system of modern thought not in nature or tradition but in the private interiority of his consciousness, on a clear and distinct idea, arguably the most famous one-liner in the history of philosophy: *cogito, ergo sum*—I think, therefore I am.[1]

We have come to call this the Cartesian approach—subjectivist, rationalist, suspicious. It has had a major influence not only on the modern physical sciences but also on the typically modern understanding of religion. When Immanuel Kant (1724–1804) sought to articulate a religion "within the limits of reason alone," he appealed to an inner, subjective sense, the moral imperative that we must follow our ethical duty. All of religion—liturgy, ritual, biblical narrative, dogmas, creeds—can and should be reduced to this interior, subjective experience, he said. It is the rock upon which the whole structure is built. Similarly, in Hegel (1770–1831) we find a sharp distinction between religion on the one hand (tainted by imagination and particularity) and true philosophy on the other (beautifully abstract and rational).[2]

Descartes has shaped modernity in his subjectivism and in his rationalism. But there have been serious consequences of this for how we relate to our bodies. When Descartes' self-authenticating, *thinking* subject is the cornerstone of everything, all sense experience is to be doubted. And because the body belongs to the realm of the senses, the indubitable *ego* has no necessary connection to the body. The source and ground of the characteristically modern philosophy are therefore literally disincarnate.

The Cartesian mind is removed from muscle, bone, movement, and blood. Here is born the mind-body dualism that has shaped modern philosophy, influenced contemporary theology, and rendered suspect the bodily gestures and practices that make up the devotions of faith in ordinary Christian life. Here is born the modern tendency to *explain* everything, to make religion understandable and inoffensive. And now, what is a consequence of this disincarnate Christianity? A generation fascinated by "spirituality" and often bored by church; millions who embrace the colorful embodiments of the New Age but who find Christian worship too cerebral and unimaginative.

INTRODUCTION

In her book *Honoring the Body*, Stephanie Paulsell asks

> What is this body we wish to honor? There seem to be as many descriptions of the body as there are people to describe it. The body is a friend or a traitor. A gift or a task. Something precious knit together by God's own hands or the prison house of the soul, which, according to Plato, is trapped in the body like an oyster in a shell. Most descriptions of the body tend to fall into one or two camps: some suggest that the essence of who we are is merely encased, temporarily, in a body. In other words, a body is something we *have*. Others suggest that what is essential about human being cannot be separated from our bodies. In other words, we *are* our bodies in a very fundamental way.[3]

The truth is, Paulsell reflects, that most of us do not seize once and for all on one description or the other, but move back and forth between the two. Do we inhabit a body, or is a body who we truly are? If we believe that we simply *have* a body, then the fulfillment of our bodily desires will not be placed above every other consideration; that could be a positive outcome. But we might also come to view the body as somehow distinct from who we are; that could be a negative outcome. On the other hand, if we believe that we *are* our bodies, we will very likely hold the human body in higher esteem than if we perceived of it only as the shell encasing out true self. "Such is the mystery of the body," Paulsell exclaims. "Sometimes we know that we are our bodies, that our capacity for life and death makes us who we are. At other times, we feel that we simply inhabit a vessel that is inadequate to contain all that we are."[4]

Such intellectual modesty with regard to our bodiliness is, I believe, entirely appropriate. In everything having to do with the body we are in the realm of mystery. The body is not simply a riddle that we can solve with enough concerted *thinking*. It presents us with mystery in two significant ways. First, we don't understand everything about the body, beginning with our own body. While the body reveals itself to thought, it also conceals itself from our minds. How many times have we wondered aloud to others with reference to a skin condition or neurological complaint, "I wish I knew what is going on with my body...." The means by which we reveal ourselves to others and unite lovingly with others is laced with ambiguity. Second, we cannot simply step out of our bodies like a jump-suit, as though it were something we *have* rather than also what we *are*. The more we attempt to objectify the body and write it on the board like an algebra problem to be solved, the more we risk self-distortion. Further, our bodies are not only something to be disciplined by our minds and wills; they also instruct and discipline *us* in often humbling ways. Like the adult who limps from bed to the bathroom after an over-exerted outing, we either bring an attitude of receptive attention to our bodies or pay for it the day after.[5]

While biblical faith does not entirely lift the veil of mystery from our embodied being, it is by no means silent on the question either. For Jews and Christians alike, the opening chapter of the Book of Genesis affirms that we are created male and female in God's own image and that the body reflects God's own goodness. To find the significant New Testament reference points, one need look no further than the major festivals of Christian faith. In the festival of Christmas, it is precisely God's becoming *flesh* in a historical person, Jesus of Nazareth, that is celebrated. In the feast of the transfiguration on Mount Tabor, Jesus is not only revealed as the fulfillment of the law and the prophets, but he also gives us a glimpse into our own human dignity and destiny. At Easter, Christians celebrate Jesus' *bodily* resurrection from the dead. And forty days later, on the feast of Jesus' ascension into heaven, Christians find a foreshadowing of the entry of their own embodied nature into the intimate embrace of God's trinitarian life. Ten days after the ascension comes Pentecost: the Holy Spirit, God's own life, is given to vessels of clay, this mortal flesh. In short, there is every indication that salvation does not mean getting *out* of this skin, but being transfigured and glorified *in* it. A spiritual body, yes, but a *body*. No wonder, then, that the apostle Paul wrote, "Do you not know that your body is a temple of the Holy Spirit...? Therefore glorify God in your body"[6]

This biblical legacy is fine wine, but alas, Christianity has poured copious water into its wine and resisted the radical nature of its own good news where the body is concerned. On the one hand, it has the highest theological evaluation of the body among all the religions of the world, and on the other hand, it has given little attention to the body's role in the spiritual life in positive terms. High theology; low practice.

I came to the realization of this discrepancy indirectly. It is a story that I must briefly tell in order to share with you the matrix from which this collection of reflections evolved. While doing research for a book eventually titled *Prayer of Heart and Body: Meditation and Yoga as Christian Spiritual Practice* (Paulist Press, 1995), I was amazed to find how little reflection existed from a Christian perspective on the positive role of the body in the spiritual life. The same held true for Christian reflection on spiritual practices directly engaging the body that were being imported from Eastern religions. Eight million people in the United States were reportedly, at that time, practicing yoga (now fifteen million, according to *Time* magazine). But with one or two exceptions, the only two books I could find (now out of print) were published in the early 1960s by the French Benedictine J. M. Déchanet.[7]

In the course of the 1990s, I was also leading Prayer of Heart and Body retreats for people who, like myself, had found great benefit in yoga and meditation but who were looking to integrate their practice into their spiritual lives as Christians. A number of people who made these retreats became sufficiently motivated to become yoga teachers themselves so they could, in turn, bring this integrative approach into Christian settings in their own towns and cities.

At the beginning of the new millennium, I began receiving requests from these retreatants-become-teachers: Could we come together to reflect with one another in the light of our experience, to share notes on where more theological work is needed, to support each other? In response, I put out an invitation to those in this small-but-growing network to come together for a five-day period in July 2001 at Mount Paul, a retreat center owned by my religious community in Oak Ridge, New Jersey.

Eighteen yoga teachers and practitioners from across the United States and Canada dovetailed their summer schedules to participate. Among them were two Catholic priests, two Protestant ministers, three psychotherapists, a medical doctor, a spiritual director, and a retreat-center program director. Roughly half had graduate degrees in theology. If the absence of published Christian reflection on yoga is any indication, it may have been the first time in the North American context that a group committed to both yoga and meditation came together for several days to reflect on their experience precisely as Christians.

Several of the participants made presentations to the group as a stimulus to discussion and sharing among ourselves. These presentations were the seminal form for the chapters in this book. But it is not a book about yoga as such. It also addresses those who cycle, swim, ski, jog, dance, play ball, engage in manual labor, and make love.

The central issue and focus of this volume is the place of the body in the spiritual life. The topic is an important one for all those who practice some physical discipline, yoga or otherwise, that directly engages the body, as well as for those who do not. It relates to all those on the planet who walk upright on two legs and who have the capacity for self-reflection. In short, the question is this: What are the implications of our embodied being for the ways we go to God?

That question, we have found, is like a self-inflating air mattress. Once you unfold it and roll it out, it expands before your very eyes. You start off thinking just in terms of the individual human body, but your theological reflection soon makes you realize that individuals are part of a larger community, and therefore you must deal with whether the individual's practice is connected in any salutary way to the social body. And once you begin to look at the needs of the community, you come face to face with the environment—the earth-body—in which the community lives and its relationship to it.

Four of the six chapters in this book were written by participants in the Oak Ridge gathering. Fr. James Wiseman, OSB, provides some highlights (and lowlights) in a brief overview of the history of Christian attitudes toward the body. I stake out a foundation for a positive approach to the body in Christian spirituality today and then look at the body language of faith. Casey Rock reflects on her experience as a yoga teacher and practitioner and compares it to what she experiences in the contemporary parish. Rev. Jim Dickerson addresses the critical issue of the individual member's solidarity with the needs of the larger, social body. And Dr. Jim Hall takes our awareness to another level, holding up to us the dust from which we come and to which we shall return, and reminding us that in the scheme of God's creation, the "body" to which we belong is much larger than that to which we generally revert. How do our exercises, both physical and spiritual, help us care for all that is, like us, embodied? The implications of a spirituality of embodiment are far reaching.

In the Celtic tradition, there is a sense of the mystery of God being revealed through two "texts"—through holy scripture, the "little" book, and through creation, the "great" book.

INTRODUCTION

Our life and the whole life of creation have been uttered into being by God, so we listen for intimations of the divine deep within all that has been created. The human body is a sacred text within the larger text of creation.[8] As the encompassing sweep of this collection of essays shows, we have attempted to listen attentively to both these texts in contributing to a spirituality that resonates with the preoccupations of our times.

Thomas Ryan

Notes

1. Robert Barron, *The Strangest Way: Walking the Christian Path* (Maryknoll, NY: Orbis, 2002), 20.

2. Ibid., 20, 23.

3. Stephanie Paulsell, *Honoring the Body* (New York: Jossey-Bass, 2002), 16.

4. Ibid., 18, 20.

5. Luke Timothy Johnson, "A Disembodied 'Theology of the Body'" in *Commonweal* (January 26, 2001), 13.

6. See 1 Corinthians 6:12–20.

7. J. M. Déchanet, *Christian Yoga* (London: Burns and Oates, 1960) and *Yoga in Ten Lessons* (New York: Simon and Schuster, 1965).

8. J. Philip Newell, *Echo of the Soul: The Sacredness of the Human Body* (Harrisburg, PA: Morehouse, 2000), 15.

The Body in Spiritual Practice: Some Historical Points of Reference

James Wiseman

The topic of the body in spiritual practice is vast. I will therefore circumscribe my treatment in two principal ways. First, while not completely ignoring insights from other religious traditions, I will focus on the one I know best—Christianity—and second, I will deal mainly with three particular points within this tradition: (1) the understanding of the body as such; (2) the role of the body in prayer and meditation; and (3) the body in the context of marriage. In all three cases, I will discuss past attitudes and then describe how these attitudes have changed in recent (or in some cases not-so-recent) times.

Before turning to these specific points, I should say something about one term in the title of this chapter. "Spiritual" is a word that has long been suspect in many circles insofar as it was understood to imply a severely other-worldly, anti-corporeal approach to life on earth. Scholars working today in the field of spirituality—itself a relative newcomer among the various academic disciplines—have labored mightily to avoid that connotation. Christian writers have done this mainly by seeing spirituality as related to living under the guidance of the divine spirit, the Holy Spirit. Scripture scholars point out, for example, that when St. Paul in his various letters contrasts "the spiritual person" with one who is "carnal" or "fleshly," the distinction is not between the incorporeal and the corporeal but rather between those whose whole being and life are ordered or influenced by the Spirit of God and those whose attitudes and behavior are opposed to God's Spirit. In this chapter about "the body in spiritual practice," I am therefore not attempting to forge some union between two realities that are diametrically opposed ("body" and "spirit") but am rather trying to show how a proper use and understanding of the body is in fact an integral part of a genuinely spiritual or Spirit-filled life.

Some Christian Understandings of the Body

How has the human body been understood within the Christian tradition? In the gospels, the body (*soma* in Greek) is not a concept of primary importance. When mentioned at all, it is sometimes distinguished from the soul, as when Jesus says: "Do not fear those who kill the body but cannot kill the soul; rather fear him who can destroy both soul and body in hell" (Matt 10:28). There is nothing especially derogatory about the body in such a saying, though there is clearly a certain subordination of body to soul in terms of importance. So, too, in St. Paul's letters the body is by no means seen as something evil. Indeed, for Paul *soma* is often spoken of as being exceedingly precious, as when he writes: "Do you not know that your body is a temple of the Holy Spirit within you…and that you are not your own? For you have been bought with a price. Therefore glorify God in your body" (1 Cor 6:19–20).

Nevertheless, there are also some Pauline passages that are less positive, since he regrets that bodily life here on earth inevitably prevents his being fully present with the Lord. Paul accordingly writes to the Corinthians, "So we are always confident; even though we know that while we are at home in the body we are away from the Lord—for we walk by faith, not by sight. Yes, we do have confidence, and we would rather be away from the body and at home with the Lord" (2 Cor 5:6–8).

This ambivalence about the body—its being a temple of the Holy Spirit on the one hand but an obstacle to full union with Christ on the other—has been present in the Christian tradition down the centuries. At times, however, the negative aspect became far more accentuated than it ever was in St. Paul's letters. This evolution, or better, this "devolution," was in large measure due to influence by certain strands of Greek philosophy on Christian writers. Although it would be grossly unfair to portray Plato as unambiguously anti-corporeal, and although the major Christian authors who respected his thought did not appropriate it in an uncritical way, certain passages from Plato's own works and from those of some of his disciples did influence

3

the Christian understanding of the body. The so-called Platonic dualism between soul and body is especially evident in certain parts of the *Phaedo*, as when Plato has Socrates say:

> So long as we keep to the body and our soul is contaminated with this imperfection, there is no chance of our ever attaining satisfactorily to our object, which we assert to be truth....It seems that so long as we are alive, we shall continue closest to knowledge if we avoid as much as we can all contact and association with the body, except when they are absolutely necessary, and instead of allowing ourselves to become infected with its nature, purify ourselves from it until God himself gives us deliverance.[1]

Philo of Alexandria, the Jewish philosopher who lived at the time of Christ and had considerable influence on later Christian writers like Origen and Clement of Alexandria, took up this Platonic strain. Like St. Paul, he too used the imagery of the athlete, but in a way that was more denigrating toward the body. He writes, for example: "The athlete refers all to the good health of the body, and, body-lover that he is, would abandon the soul itself for its sake; but the philosopher...cares for the soul and disregards that which is in reality a corpse, the body, with the sole aim that the best part of him, his soul, may not be wronged by an evil thing, the cadaver to which it is bound."[2]

Under this kind of influence from Hellenic thought, it is not surprising that Clement of Alexandria, who died early in the third century, should have taught that the Savior, Jesus Christ, did not have a human body just like our own but rather a heavenly one that was free of all bodily needs and passions. For Clement, even the advanced followers of Christ, those whom he called the genuine Gnostics, did not experience such passions as anger, fear, or lust but underwent merely those "affections that exist for the maintenance of the body, such as hunger, thirst, and the like." And Christ, he taught, did not undergo even these affections. Clement writes: "In the case of the Savior, it would be ludicrous [to suppose] that the body, as a body, demanded the necessary aids for its duration. For He ate not for the sake of the body, which was kept together by a holy energy, but in order that it might not enter into the minds of those who were with Him to entertain a different opinion of Him....But He was entirely impassible *(apathes)*, inaccessible to any movement of feeling—either pleasure or pain."[3]

About forty years after Clement died, and further south in the same land of Egypt, was born a man who, though unlettered, became even more influential than Clement. Anthony of the Desert, generally reckoned as the founder of the Christian monastic movement, undertook the life of a desert solitary after consulting with a number of ascetics who lived on the outskirts of villages near the Nile River. After spending several decades in quite complete seclusion, he emerged at the urging of others and quickly attracted a fervent band of disciples. The *Life of Anthony*, written by his friend St. Athanasius after the hermit's death, became one of the earliest best sellers in Christian literature. Much of Athanasius's portrayal of Anthony is endearing. He tells us that if someone who had never met the man wanted to locate him in a crowd of monks, he had only to spot the person whose face was radiant with joy. Despite an austere lifestyle, Anthony is said to have lived to the remarkably advanced age of a hundred and five and to have been so healthy at the time of his death as still to have all of his teeth.

Clearly this saint's asceticism—his fastings and nighttime vigils—did not in any sense produce a lugubrious, emaciated specter but rather a vibrant person full of joy in the Holy Spirit. From our contemporary perspective, however, there are also darker sides to what Athanasius writes. At one point he says: "When [Anthony] was about to eat and sleep and provide for the other needs of the body, shame overcame him as he thought of the spiritual nature of the soul. Often when about to partake of food with many other monks, the thought of spiritual food came upon him and he would beg to be excused and went a long way from them, thinking that he should be ashamed to be seen eating by others."[4] Two chapters later, Athanasius writes that Anthony never bathed and that no one ever saw him undressed, nor did anyone ever look upon his naked body until he died and was buried.

Nine centuries later, the saint whom many consider the most Christlike of all—Francis of Assisi—was similarly ambivalent about caring for his body, though with effects much more deleterious to his health. In Thomas of Celano's *Second Life* of the saint, there is a striking account of an exchange that Francis had with an unnamed friar. Francis was now near the end of his life, broken in body largely as a result of the severity of the mortifications he had practiced for so many years. Thomas says that on this occasion, when it seemed proper to the brothers to apply some soothing remedies to the saint's body, Francis first sought counsel of this one friar, expressing the fear that by accepting the treatment he would be indulging his body too much.

The wise brother, after calling the saint's attention to the fact that his body had served him faithfully for so many years, then asked: "Where then, Father, is your generosity, where are your kindness and discretion? Is this a worthy way to repay a faithful friend—to accept a kindness willingly, but when the giver is in need not to repay him as he deserves?" After some further conversation along these lines, Francis came to agree and addressed his body with these words: "Rejoice, brother body, and forgive me, for, behold, I now gladly fulfill your desires; I hasten to give heed to your complaints." Thomas of Celano adds, however, that Francis's change of heart had come too late. His body had already collapsed in every part, and death came shortly thereafter.[5]

One further aspect of a negative understanding of the body in the Christian tradition concerns what St. Benedict refers to in chapter eight of his monastic Rule, when he says that between the two early-morning services of Vigils and Lauds there should be a short interval "during which the brothers may go out [from the oratory] for the needs of nature." The functions of bodily excretion have often been considered altogether unseemly within the Christian tradition. One of the later reform movements within Benedictine monasticism itself was the seventeenth-century Trappist reform. Although, contrary to popular belief, Trappist monks never took a vow of silence, they did practice silence in a very strict way, so that until quite recently they regularly used sign language except when they had to converse with either their abbot or their confessor. There was, of course, a sign for "bathroom" (or "toilet"), a compound sign that means "shame-house." That bit of sign language is a sad commentary on what the body and bodily functions have often signified within the Christian tradition. Let me, however, turn now to show the other side of the coin, for which I am happily not limited only to recent works.

Positive Appreciation of the Body

Among the really wonderful women writers in the history of Christian spirituality was the fourteenth-century English anchoress Julian of Norwich. Her *Showings* (or *Revelations*) was quite appropriately the very first volume published in that eminently successful and still-ongoing series of The Classics of Western Spirituality from Paulist Press. In the sixth chapter of the Long Text of her work there is the following passage:

> The highest form of prayer is to the goodness of God, which comes down to us to our humblest needs. It gives life to our souls and makes them live and grow in grace and virtue. It is nearest in nature and promptest in grace, for it is the same grace which the soul seeks and always will, until we truly know our God, who has enclosed us all in himself.
>
> A man walks upright, and the food in his body is shut in as if in a well-made purse. When the time of

his necessity comes, the purse is opened and then shut again, in most seemly fashion. And it is God who does this, as it is shown when he says that he comes down to us in our humblest needs. For he does not despise what he has made, nor does he disdain to serve us in the simplest natural functions of our bodies....For as the body is clad in the cloth, and the flesh in the skin, and the bones in the flesh, and the heart in the trunk, so are we, soul and body, clad and enclosed in the goodness of God.[6]

The editor of one modern translation of Julian's Middle English text notes that this passage, "earthy yet discreet," does not appear in one of the two extant manuscript versions of the Long Text,[7] but it is very likely that Julian herself did write it and that it was omitted from one manuscript only by a squeamish copyist, for it does bridge the sense from the previous paragraph in a way that is typical of Julian.

In so writing, Julian anticipated by six centuries the positive appreciation of the body that came to expression in one of the most important documents of the Second Vatican Council, *Gaudium et Spes,* the Pastoral Constitution on the Church in the Modern World. Its very first chapter, on the dignity of the human person, says the following about our essential nature:

The human person, though made of body and soul, is a unity. Through one's very bodily condition one sums up in oneself the elements of the material world, which are thus brought to their highest perfection and can raise their voice in praise freely given to the Creator. For this reason, one may not despise one's bodily life. Rather one is obliged to regard one's body as good and to hold it in honor, since God has created it and will raise it up on the last day.[8]

Much more could be said about various kinds of self-discipline called for in properly caring for the body: avoiding overeating (especially in light of recent findings about the high percentage of Americans who are unhealthily overweight), going easy on junk food, and making sure that one gets enough sleep. Cornell University psychologist and sleep expert James Maas recently said that more than half of the population of the United States is carrying a substantial sleep debt, especially prevalent among adolescents and young adults, who are the age group involved in most fall-asleep automobile crashes. Maas believes that for most people eight hours is the minimum amount of sleep needed per night, the period between the seventh and eighth hour being especially important as the time when, in his words, the mind best "repairs itself, grows new connections, and puts it all together."[9] The traditional motto of Jesuit education, *mens sana in corpore sano* (a sound mind in a sound body), in many ways encapsulates a holistic spirituality, one that cares for the body as a precious gift from God instead of neglecting it or stifling its development through imprudent mortifications.

The Role of the Body in Prayer and Meditation

Even the little I have written thus far should be enough to indicate that genuine spirituality is concerned with much more than the devotional practices of prayer and meditation, even though there may have been a time when spirituality was practically equated with such exercises. But if prayer is not the whole of spiritual living, it is an important part of it, and here too we have some ancient antecedents.

Of the books about prayer written in the early or middle part of the twentieth century, one was by Cardinal Giacomo Lercaro, archbishop of Bologna, and published under the title *Metodi di Orazione Mentale,* translated into English as *Methods of Mental Prayer.* Several Trappist abbots published books with similar titles: Dom Vital Lehodey's *The Ways of Mental Prayer* and Dom Godefroid Bélorgey's *The Practice of Mental Prayer.* Note that the very term "mental prayer" conveys a sense that there is no particular role for the body in one's practice of prayer. Indeed, the last-named author, in line with a long tradition, defined prayer as "an elevation of the soul to God" and began his book with the following words:

> Prayer is a divine colloquy arising from the intimate spiritual relationships which exist in faith and in charity between God and the soul. It depends upon God and the soul. The soul must use its intellect and will to know God, to love Him, and to converse supernaturally

with Him. But it can only do this when…it is moved and aided by divine grace….For true prayer, both God and the soul must play their parts in harmony and union.[10]

To be sure, there is nothing in this or similar books that expresses positive disdain for the body, but the overall neglect of any reference to the body is telling, giving the impression that the prayerful person at his or her best is more an angel than a human being. Some early ascetics even claimed explicitly to be trying to live an angelic life on earth.

Nowadays the very language used by writers on prayer tends to be quite different. The term "mental prayer" is generally avoided, and those contemporary writers who do look to the past for insights and inspiration pass over authors like Lehodey and Bélorgey in favor of much older writers like Gregory Palamas, the fourteenth-century defender of the Eastern Orthodox monks of Mount Athos against their critics. Gregory's own sources were monks like Nicephorus the Hesychast and Gregory of Sinai, many of whose writings are now available in books with such titles as *Writings from the Philokalia: On Prayer of the Heart*. In our own time, Bishop Kallistos Ware and other Eastern Orthodox writers have emphasized the intimate role of the body in this kind of prayer, whose method has three main features:

(1) A particular bodily posture is adopted: [one is] seated, with the head and shoulders bowed, and the gaze directed toward the place of the heart or the

navel. (2) The speed of the breathing is slowed down, and the words of the Jesus Prayer ["Lord Jesus Christ, Son of God, have mercy on me"] are coordinated with the inhalation and exhalation of the breath....(3) Through a discipline of "inner exploration," attention is concentrated upon specific psychosomatic centers,...especially the heart.[11]

The widespread practice of this form of prayer today, not at all confined to the borders of Eastern Orthodoxy, is an indication that persons are more apt to adopt a way of praying that has a recognized role for the body as over against methods that come across as too severely mental.

Bishop Ware and others have noted that this "prayer of the heart" shows striking similarities with certain techniques used in yoga, though it would be difficult to find proof of direct influence. One recent book that discusses both ways is entitled *Prayer of Heart and Body*, by the Paulist priest Thomas Ryan. After giving a clear introduction to the practice of the prayer of the heart in part one of his book, in parts two and three Fr. Ryan turns to a consideration of ways in which one could use yoga to foster what he terms "prayer of the body." His book includes illustrations of some basic yogic *asanas* (that is, postures) that one could correlate with the prayerful recitation of a traditional text like the Lord's Prayer. I certainly do not want to imply that yogic techniques are at all necessary for a deep prayer life. Nevertheless, it is worth hearing some words of a health-care worker whom

Fr. Ryan quotes in the chapter entitled "How Yoga Can Help a Christian Pray." This woman said:

> For me, yoga and prayer are inextricably linked. When I perform the various asanas, I am praying with my body. These series of physical exercises help me to achieve a sense of stillness and peace in which prayer becomes easier and the nagging worries of the day seem less urgent....At the end of many yoga classes I have been overcome with a profound sense of awe, gratitude and adoration. The transcendent God seems somehow closer....

She then goes on to provide a word of caution:

> It is precisely because yoga is a spiritual practice that I have always taken seriously those Christian leaders who warn of its dangers. Yoga is a technique that can help prayer, but Christian prayer is never merely a technique to achieve a state of transcendence.... Although grace is a gift that no method can manufacture, I feel that yoga disposes me to pray more tranquilly and to be open to whatever gifts God may wish to give.[12]

This, I believe, is very balanced and sound advice. Many Christians today have begun exploring yoga and have thereby come to sense something of the value that that woman found in its practice, especially how it helped her "pray with her body."

The Body in the Context of Marriage

Finally, I wish to consider the place of the body in the context of marriage. That the body is central goes without saying; that this centrality has often been very problematic in the Christian tradition is little short of tragic. Marriage itself was long regarded as objectively inferior to celibacy, a position based on such scriptural texts as Jesus' praise of those who renounce marriage for the sake of the Kingdom (Matt 19:12) and St. Paul's clear preference for celibacy on the grounds that married persons are anxious about "the things of the world" and how they may please their spouse and so are "divided," while the unmarried need be anxious only "about the affairs of the Lord" and so "may be holy in body and spirit" (1 Cor 7:32–34).

Certainly there is not the slightest hint in such passages that marriage is evil, and in fact the early and medieval Church strove mightily against heretical movements that claimed it was. Nevertheless, theologians like St. Augustine (354–430) did develop views about marriage that are quite removed from the Church's teaching today. I am by no means an "Augustine basher." Indeed, I consider his *Confessions* one of the most impressive and inspiring books I have ever read. Even his treatment of sexuality and marriage has been interpreted rather sympathetically by some leading women scholars of our day, such as Mary T. Clark and Margaret Miles.[13] But I am surely not alone in cringing at those passages in his voluminous work in which sexual intercourse, the most intimate communion possible between husband and wife, is said to be inescapably sinful,

15

excusable only with a view to a desired outcome of progeny. He said, for example, in one of his sermons:

> My brethren, understand the sense of Scripture concerning our ancient fathers, whose sole design in their marriage was to have children by their wives.... Whoever exceeds the limits which this rule prescribes for the fulfillment of this end of marriage acts contrary to the very contract by which he took his wife. The contract is read in the presence of all the attesting witnesses, and an express clause is there that they marry "for the procreation of children," and this is called the marriage contract. If it was not for this that wives were given and taken to wife, what father could without blushing give up his daughter to the lust of any man?...Nevertheless, if [the couple] cannot restrain themselves, let them require what is due, and let them not go to any others than those from whom it is due....If they exceed the bounds of the marriage contract, let them at least not exceed those of conjugal fidelity. Is it not a sin in married persons to exact from one another more than what this design of the "procreation of children" renders necessary? It is doubtless a sin, though a venial one. (Sermon 51 in the Maurist edition, sec. 22)

Or again, in his *Soliloquies*, when Augustine presents himself as being in conversation with Reason personified, there is this exchange: Reason asks, "What about a wife? Would you not be delighted by a fair, modest, and obedient wife…?" Augustine replies: "No matter how much you choose to portray and endow her with all good qualities, I have decided that there is nothing I should avoid so much as marriage. I know nothing which brings the manly mind down from the heights more than a woman's caresses and that joining of bodies without which one cannot have a wife."[14]

When one considers that probably no writer apart from St. Paul has had more influence in the Christian West than Augustine, one can readily see what obstacles lay in the way of those who have sought to develop a more positive understanding of what Augustine calls "that joining of bodies without which one cannot have a wife." The change has, nevertheless, come about, not least because of the way some husbands and wives have honestly described how sexual intercourse has in fact fostered their love for one another and for God. As one fine example of what I mean, consider the following words of Joseph and Lois Bird:

> Prayer is the directing of one's thoughts and actions toward God;… if we think of conjugal prayer in these terms, we should have little difficulty recognizing the marital union as a profound prayer. In turning to each other in sexual love, the couple turn toward God. Their act of love becomes a profession of faith, and of hope, as they give themselves in cooperation with [God's] plan….

[Nevertheless,] recognizing on an intellectual level the holiness of the marital union and *experiencing* spirituality in the conjugal act are not the same thing. Most Christian couples, we feel sure, would agree that marital relations are blessed by God, but few can say they experience a benediction in the act. Why? Probably, two reasons: First of all, marital sexuality is seldom presented as a spiritual encounter. As children, we learned only a negative view. Parents, in their concern with the dangers of sexual immorality, stressed sin, and little else....But there is another, more important reason. Discovering the presence of Christ in the sexual union is a reward which is found not in a blinding flash of insight, but through gradual awareness, paralleling the growth of husband and wife toward the goal of mutual sanctity. It is the marriage, the total relationship, which must mature....The *whole* marriage grows, or no growth takes place. Husband and wife come to *know* Christ, to *love* Him, and to *see* Him in their sexual union, as they strive to *know, love,* and *see* each other.[15]

Among other things, this kind of experience of married persons also qualifies St. Paul's words about spouses being "divided" because they are anxious about pleasing their spouse. The apostle's implication is that seeking to please one's spouse distracts a person from the Pauline ideal of pleasing the Lord, of glorifying God in *all* that one does. Couples like the one just quoted simply do not experience that kind of disjunction. Loving each other, even in what is physically the most intimate way, *includes* their loving God. This insight, which was once expressed in a more general way by the great theologian Karl Rahner in his reflections on the unity of the two great commandments of love of God and love of neighbor,[16] is of particular importance for married persons.

This brief overview of some historical points of reference concerning the body in Christian spirituality has set the stage for the chapters that follow. There have clearly been major advances toward a more positive appreciation of the body when compared with some attitudes in the past. Harsh mortification of the body as though it were some kind of obstacle to genuine holiness or wholeness is no longer advocated. The role of the body in prayer and meditation is today regularly understood as being integral to spiritual practice, while spouses more and more commonly see their married love for one another as inclusive of their love of God. All of this reflects a welcome return to a more gospel-centered spirituality, in the footsteps of the one who said that our salvation depends on the way we meet the bodily needs of others—feeding the hungry, giving drink to the thirsty, and in these and similar ways ministering to the Lord Jesus himself (Matt 25:31–46).

Notes

1. Plato, *Phaedo* 66b–67a.
2. Philo, *Allegories of the Laws* 3.72.
3. Clement of Alexandria, *Stromata*, ch. 9.

4. Athanasius, *Life of Anthony*, ch. 45.

5. Thomas of Celano, *Second Life of St. Francis*, ch. 160.

6. Julian of Norwich, *Showings*, trans. Edmund Colledge, OSA, and James Walsh, SJ (New York: Paulist Press, 1978), 185–86.

7. John Skinner, ed. and trans. of Julian of Norwich, *Revelation of Love* (New York: Doubleday, Image Books, 1996), 13n10.

8. *Gaudium et Spes*, no. 14. Translation slightly altered for inclusive language.

9. Quoted in U-Wire reports, January 19, 2001.

10. Dom Godefroid Bélorgey, OCSO, *The Practice of Mental Prayer* (Westminster, MD: Newman, 1952),

11. Kallistos Ware, "Ways of Prayer and Contemplation. 1. Eastern," in *Christian Spirituality: Origins to the Twelfth Century*, ed. Bernard McGinn and John Meyendorff (New York: Crossroad, 1985), 408–9.

12. Pat O'Rourke, quoted by Thomas Ryan, CSP, in *Prayer of Heart and Body: Meditation and Yoga as Christian Spiritual Practice* (New York: Paulist Press, 1995), 183.

13. Mary T. Clark, RSCJ, *Augustine* (Washington, DC: Georgetown University Press, 1994), 126–27; Margaret Miles, *Desire and Delight: A New Reading of Augustine's Confessions* (New York: Crossroad, 1992), 68–71.

14. Augustine, *Soliloquies* 1.10.

15. Joseph W. Bird and Lois F. Bird, *The Freedom of Sexual Love* (Garden City, NY: Doubleday, 1967), 149–51.

16. Karl Rahner, "Reflections on the Unity of the Love of Neighbor and the Love of God," in *Theological Investigations*, vol. 6, trans. Karl-H. and Boniface Kruger (Baltimore: Helicon, 1969), 231–49.

2.

Toward a Positive Spirituality of the Body

Thomas Ryan

Not long ago, the geography of spirituality was the interior or inner life, the "life of the soul." It meant having to do with our "spiritual" life or life of private prayer with God. The basic premise was that we grow holier by our personal prayer. Spiritual books dealt with realities outside the realm of ordinary human experience.

Today, Christian spirituality is understood as Christian *life* in the Spirit. It relates to our whole existence before God and amid the created world: prayer, work, play, time with family and friends. It is the human spirit being grasped, sustained, and transformed by the Holy Spirit through all the circumstances of our lives. We have broadened our understanding of what it means to grow in holiness. "Spiritual" growth and "human" growth partake of the same reality. Prayer is important because it puts me in direct contact with God, the source of my growth, but it is just one of the ways in which I grow in holiness. I also grow through the experience of self-discovery and interaction with others, through the experience of struggle and pain and loss.

In other words, contemporary spirituality is more holistic. Its main focus is not the interior journey or the life of the soul narrowly understood. In this new territory we do not make rivals of soul and body, spirit and flesh, church and world, sacred and profane. Christian spirituality is being conformed to the person of Christ and being united in communion with God and others through the full range of human experience.

The recurring influence of dualism does not make this an academic question. In a dualistic worldview, one's body and one's spirit are in a forced marriage, and as soon as the spirit can get out of the marriage, the better. When that is one's worldview, one's body is more foe than friend. When St. Paul addressed these words to the Corinthians, they listened to them against a background of dualism: "Do you not know that your bodies are members of Christ?...Or do you not know that your body is a temple of the Holy Spirit within you, which you have from God, and that you are not your own? For you were bought with a price; therefore glorify God in your body" (1 Cor 6:15, 19, 20).

We evidently needed some effective convincing with regard to our own inestimable value. That perhaps is what influenced John the Evangelist in his Prologue to choose the unique phrasing that the Word of God became *flesh*. The expression is both graphic and dramatic. God becomes one of us, a living being of flesh and blood, experiencing life in this world just as we experience it—eating and drinking, working and resting, touching and being touched, suffering and dying.

It was not a masquerade party or playacting. It was not something that could ever be taken back or undone. It was, we might say, a serious commitment. In the face of our devaluations of the flesh that embodies God and the earth which is God's home, God sent us a message: from now on, I am identified with this bodiliness, this fleshiness, this materiality, this sensuality, this worldliness, this passion.

If ever we wanted to trade in this bodily existence for another kind, in the face of that message we no longer have any ground to do so. Where we are and what we are is now the intimate habitat of God. If ever we approached life in this world as some rehearsal, some kind of warm-up in preparation for the real thing in another world, the incarnation—the enfleshment of God—demands that we revise that assessment in favor of recognizing the inherent value of our embodied earthly life. In the birth-event at Bethlehem, the Eternal Word of God took on the world as part of himself in the body of Jesus of Nazareth. The stuff of material creation quite literally became the body of God. Henceforth, there is no basis for dismissing this world as some second-rate practice field for the real life in heaven. The Word of God becoming flesh means that there is no practice and nothing is second rate. Life in this world is already shot through with divinity, with the very life of God.

If we wish to devise a spirituality for ourselves whereby the spiritual minded must be other-worldly and whereby spiritual growth is measured by antipathy toward this world, this body, this life, then we will have to fly in the face of the very example God has given us. We have not been burdened with this world and this flesh in order that we might weasel our way out. Rather, we have been gifted with this world and these bodies because this is where God dwells. All flesh is holy and the ground of all human endeavors is sacred. It is in these bodies that we will work out our salvation. Human bodies are part of God's image and the means through which absolutely everything we can learn about God must come to us.

God, seeing our difficulty because of sin to move toward God, in compassion moves toward us. Where do we meet? In the body—the body of Christ. Jesus is the embodiment of the love of God for human beings. Jesus is the meeting place for God and humans in the flesh. The Spirit falls upon Mary, and the Word becomes flesh. The same Spirit falls upon us, and we become members of the Body of Christ in his Church and meet God there in sensual, material signs of water, oil, bread, and wine.

Note that throughout the ages we have not described ourselves as an assembly of believers in abstract terms. We have not called the Church the "spirit of Christ" but the "Body of Christ." And the responsibilities we have outlined for ourselves are described as the *corporal* works of mercy, each one relating to the concrete care of individual members of that body by other members. We engage in these works because we recognize the divine presence of God in the embodied being of the other.

Today, whether we are reflecting on masculine and feminine socialization, sexuality and spirituality, images of God, the place and person of Jesus, anthropology, ethics, or current pastoral challenges and possibilities, we come back to a re-evaluation of the body as the locus of our likeness to the divine. Women in particular have been challenging the dualisms of western theology, rooted in the Neoplatonism of early Christian thought that set material and spiritual realities in contradistinction to one another, by asserting that our experience of God and ways of knowing the holy are the same as our mode of knowing all other things. That mode is sensuality.[1]

Decades of socialization, dualistic anthropologies, and patriarchal theologies have conditioned both women and men to view the body as more of a liability than an asset in the search for the holy. It is predominantly the mystics who have offered an experience of sensuality as a way of knowing God. For Julian of Norwich it is precisely in our sensuality that we are "oned" with God: "That worshipful city that our Lord Jesus sitteth in, it is our sensuality, in which he is enclosed. And our kindly substance is enclosed in Jesus; sitting, with the blessed soul of Christ, at rest in the Godhead."[2]

Opening Ourselves to God through the Experience in Our Bodies

There are many ways in our culture in which we do honor our embodied nature—from skin creams to fitness centers. But rarely do we pay attention to our bodies with the intent of opening ourselves to God *through* the experience we are having in our bodies. It is more common for us to abstain from food in order to cut a finer figure than it is for us to do so as a religious fast in order to sharpen our contact with God. It is much more common for us to pray that those who are sick will get well than to pray that their bodily experience might be a means of deepening their relationship with God. In both instances, we tend to overlook the way in which our bodily experience enables us to become more aware of God's presence and puts us in a mode of awareness where we can hear God's call coming through.

Once while I was giving talks in a town in Nova Scotia, a gentleman approached after one of the sessions and asked if I would come to his home to visit his wife who had multiple sclerosis and found it difficult to get out. But there was more going on in his house than he let on. In the back bedroom was his wife's brother, a carpenter. He was convalescing from a broken leg suffered when he fell through the roof on a job. And the man who had extended the invitation to me had taken an early retirement because of a heart condition. As I sat and talked with them, what came out was that they were all experiencing renewal in their relationships with one another. The wife and her bachelor brother had not spent much time together in many years; when he was injured, she offered him a room in her home so that he would not have to spend his days alone in bed with his leg in a cast. Her son was enjoying getting to know his uncle, and she was thrilled to reconnect with her brother. The husband was happy to have more time to assist his wife with things, and she delighted in having him around. What I saw was a free flow of grace in this network of relationships—occasioned by what each one was living in their bodies. And the rare thing is that they were conscious of this. Others might look at their situation from outside of it and say, "How sad!" But they looked at it from inside of it and said, "How wonderful!"

When we pay attention to what we are living in our bodies and how that opens us to the flow of grace in new ways, the result is renewal. If deepening our conscious communion with God is the goal, then sometimes being stripped of the busyness that fills our lives and ending up flat on our backs in bed is the best thing that could happen to us. All of a sudden we have time to listen, to reflect, to evaluate, to reorder our priorities. I no longer formulate my prayers for sick people by simply asking that so-and-so gets well. What I do ask is that their present experience—whether one of sickness or of health—be a means of deepening their relationship with God.

Suffering is never to be sought for its own sake, but it has the potential to open up God's presence to us in realms of life that were previously closed to us, opening new eyes of compassion within us. "I had never noticed people with tracheotomy tubes in their throats before having one inserted into my own chest," a friend shared with me. "Now, I am struck by the number of people I see on the streets who have one." Sometimes being healthy and well narrows both our vision of human experience and God's presence in all of it. By making sought-after idols of riches and glowing health, it's easy to lose sight of how illness and economic hardship can be circumstances of life-giving grace by making us more aware of our radical dependency upon God for everything. The first beatitude, poverty of spirit, expresses that awareness of our dependency and so contains all the other beatitudes.

Once I had a lively conversation with a group of university students around the question of "What do you think God asks of each of us? What does God call us to be?" One of them retorted, "To be good news!" As we talked, she asserted that it's not enough for us just to *read* the Good News, or even know some passages by memory; not enough, in other words, to be just *hearers* of the Word. The call is to *be* good news, to be actualizers of it.

What would that look like in practice? I asked. Suppose, she said, you run into your friend John in the supermarket while shopping. As you stand and talk, your experience of John is that he is tired and stressed. As he describes his life, the image of a treadmill comes to mind, accompanied by words like "frenetic" or "compulsive." As you walk away, you think to yourself that it would be difficult to be with John for long periods of time. He is too intense, too serious, too driven.

Later, on the street, you run into Mary and walk a couple of blocks together, chatting. She is patient at the stoplights, calm when someone brusquely crosses in front of her and cuts her off. As she tells you about her work, she sounds energized by what she does, laughs easily in recounting a recent episode, and has a cheerful word for the newsstand vendor on the corner. At the end of your day when you reflect on the events that filled it, the two encounters with John and Mary come to mind. There's no question which of these two people was like an embodied tonic, a vitamin, good news.

"How does Mary get to be that way?" I asked the group. They suggested that Mary gets enough sleep, eats a balanced diet, exercises regularly, takes time for prayer, and spends time with friends. The group effectively described someone who was "good news" because she took good care of herself, because she opened herself to God through the experiences in her body across all the activities of her day.

Their idealized cameo underscores how it is the quality of our presence that counts most in our interactions with people. It is the overflow of an interior reality. When we live like Mary even to an extent, our range of humanity, our awareness, is expanded. The potential God gave us has been actively taken hold of and worked with. People who relate to their bodies as a sacred trust and take good care of them know things in, with, and through their bodies that pass the rest of us by. What master craftsman could make such a marvel as the human body and not be disappointed when we allow it to rust? It is our task to retrieve and reinterpret the practice of honoring the body for our own age.

Honoring the Body

In her book *Honoring the Body*, Stephanie Paulsell acknowledges that Christians have inherited an ambiguous legacy about the body, affirming its goodness in bedrock beliefs, yet oftentimes experiencing the Church as a repressive institution that denies that very goodness its pleasures. She writes, however, in the conviction that there is an accumulated wisdom within our religious traditions with which we might fashion contemporary practices of honoring the body: "This is our task: to learn to see our bodies and the bodies of others through the eyes of God. To learn to see the body as both fragile and deeply blessed. To remember the body's vulnerability and to rejoice in the body as a sign of God's gracious bounty."[3]

Paulsell reflects on how we can learn to glimpse the sacredness of the body in the ordinary rituals of daily life like bathing, clothing, and touching. One of the most fundamental ways that we honor our bodies is in showering or soaking in the tub. Stripping ourselves of the clothing that provides us with a kind of protection turns it into a time of vulnerability. Bathing represents an opportunity to bless and honor the body and to perceive the sacredness at the heart of its vulnerability. In an essay in an earlier book, Paulsell recounts a story that illustrates how attention to our bodies during bathing can help to nurture a sense of the body worthy of love and care by reminding us of our creation in God's image.

> A mother of two daughters remembers that, as a teenager, she was plagued by outbreaks of acne. One day, when she felt unable to leave the house because of anguish over her face, her father led her to the bathroom and asked if he could teach her a new way to wash. He leaned over the sink and splashed water over his face, telling her, "On the first splash, say, 'In the name of the Father'; on the second, 'in the name of the Son'; and on the third, 'in the name of the Holy

30

Spirit.' Then look up into the mirror and remember that you are a child of God, full of grace and beauty."[4]

Her father's gift persisted throughout her life, and when that little girl grew up, she passed on her father's reverence for the reflection of the divine in the body to her own daughter, teaching her to sing blessings over each part of her body, and helping her remember that she is a child of God and made in God's image.

Paulsell similarly reflects on adornment or the kind of clothes we wear, observing how different occasions invoke different attire: graduates adorn themselves in academic robes that distinguish them as students who have completed a program of study; brides and grooms adorn themselves with great care and preparation to heighten the moment when they will make a gift of self to the other in their vows. The more special the occasion, the more careful we are about what we will wear and what that will say about us. How often do we think of "dressing for church" as part of our preparation for worship? What have we done to develop our own or to help cultivate in our children an aesthetic sense of what is beautiful and becoming? How we adorn ourselves can help shape our identity and heighten our experience of worshipping God with our bodies.

Touch is another way of honoring our bodies. Our culture cries out now more than ever for some understanding of how to move back and forth across the boundaries that skin establishes between us. Appropriate touch seeks to honor, not diminish, another. The woman who weeps over Jesus' feet in Luke's

Gospel and then dries them with her hair (7:36–50) teaches us that although touch can be extravagant and unexpected, its power lies in its gentleness. When Jesus washes the feet of his disciples, we see that touch is appropriate when we cross the boundaries between us from motives of generosity and not from a selfish desire to please ourselves alone.

When I offer the early morning Mass in our large church in midtown Manhattan, the people are generally sprinkled throughout the cavernous space, separated from one another by more than a pole's length. I know that some of them live alone in apartments, and I am always glad to see them get up from their places and move toward each other with hands and arms extended at the sign of peace. Especially for those who live alone, the ritual moment of "passing the peace" may represent a high point in the service because it provides a safe space within which they can touch and be touched by others, even people whom they do not know. Exchanging signs of peace with our bodies reminds us that we must touch others only in peace and love.

When a friend of mine living in Uruguay was diagnosed with intestinal cancer, a few of her friends gathered around her to provide for her needs. She had written her doctoral dissertation on "Woman as a Symbol of the Church," particularly in pregnancy when a woman is in joyous and sometimes anxious expectation. Now, as the tumor grew in her own belly, she herself looked pregnant, but it was an indication not of new life but of the end of life, not of good news but of malignancy. She felt betrayed by her own bodiliness about which she had written so beautifully. It was as though her body was mocking her. Her friends, facing their own mortality in hers and discovering a sense of their common vulnerability and fragility, sought to offer her through therapeutic touch an experience of her body as a source of comfort and not only of pain. Through the touching, her friends found themselves able to respond with compassion and acceptance rather than denial.

In her book *Nature and Other Mothers*, Brenda Peterson shares a personal experience in an essay entitled "In Praise of Skin."[5] When she was thirty-five, she broke out in a rash that left her skin peppered with red marks. She was like an adult with chicken pox, only it wasn't chicken pox; the doctors couldn't figure out what it was. She went from one medical center to another over a period of months, trying various remedies, but nothing worked. One day while she was visiting her step-grandmother, she received a more primal diagnosis: skin needs to be touched.

Her step-grandmother told her, "Your body's skin is harder working and more wide open than the human heart; it's a sad thing to see how skin gets passed over, barely touched, except in sex, or sickness, or deep trouble. Why, we pay so little mind to our skin, we might as well be living inside a foreign country." Then she proceeded to apply her own remedy: regular "treatments" of touching, massaging, and caressing Brenda's skin. Eventually the spots all faded away and her skin became healthy again.

Peterson reflects that our skin is our body's biggest organ. It breathes, filters, and protects. It is more vulnerable than the heart in that it is possible to live with one-third of your heart blocked, but if you lose one-third of your skin, you will die. It is not incidental, she observes, that the deadliest killer of our time,

AIDS, begins not with some plague-like virus invading the body, but with the breaking of the skin. Skin, she emphasizes, needs to be taken more seriously and caressed more often.

Christianity finds itself in the awkward position of trying to develop a positive theology of creation without ever having rejoiced in the human body. In theory, we have the highest theology of the body among all world religions. In practice, we are still dualistic and suspicious of anything too earthy and sensual; we live largely in our heads. And yet we believe that, in becoming flesh, God honors skin, praises skin, enters it, caresses it, embraces it. Salvation for us is not a question of escaping this skin, but of having skin glorified. That is why Jesus never preached simple immortality of the soul, but insisted on the resurrection of the body.

The Bodily Resurrection

In the resurrection we are squarely in front of the mystery of our embodied being. The apostle Paul interprets the resurrection of Jesus as a creative deed of God's mighty power. We would be mistaken to think that in Paul's own time the assertion of bodily resurrection was easily accepted. Authoritative circles among the Jews of the period did look for resurrection of the dead, but at the end of the ages. At the same time the Sadducees rejected any such hope of what the future would hold. Above all, for those educated in the culture of the Hellenistic world, the idea of a dead man rising again appeared as a folly since they regarded the body as the tomb of the soul and looked forward to liberation from it. Paul meets all these objections by pointing to the creative power of God who makes the dead live.

In common with the early Church as a whole, Paul is convinced that Christ has risen from the dead with his body. By "body" Paul understands not just one element of our makeup, different from soul, but that Christ has risen "as a whole." According to Paul, what is involved in our own death and resurrection is neither a process of complete annihilation followed by a new creation, nor a process by which the dead body is simply restored to life. What it entails is, first, "the redemption of our bodies" (Rom 8:23)—their liberation from their bondage to decay—and second, a sharing in the eternal glory of the risen Lord.

The evangelist Luke wants to bring readers to the realization that the risen Lord is certainly Jesus in his identity, but it is no longer Jesus as he was. He is transformed, changed in the way he presents himself, and he manifests a sovereign liberty in appearing and disappearing. In short, although he is still the same as regards his *identity*, he is no longer the same as regards his *reality*. In Luke's Gospel, a postresurrection Jesus appears to his disciples on the beach while they are fishing, and Luke makes a point of Jesus' continuity and identity through his wounds, with Jesus' words: "Look at my hands and feet; see that it is I myself. Touch me and see: for a ghost does not have flesh and bones as you see that I have" (24:39).

Biblical scholar Franz Mussner urges that we radically transcend the notion that the resurrected body and the earthly body are the same. Compared to the body we have at death, our resurrected body is totally other. Through a process that is different from anything we might call human experience, it is nevertheless one and the same person who undergoes and emerges from that process. Just as it was in the case of Christ, so will it be for us: the identity of the resurrected person is the same as that of the earthly person.[6]

What food for thought there is in this: that Jesus is only fully himself in becoming different! Paul uses the term "spirit-body" to characterize the risen body as one that is constituted by the Spirit that gives life. It is no longer restricted to an earthly mode of existence, that is, to flesh and blood (1 Cor 15:51), but is created anew in a "body of glory." Within this perspective there is really no place for a doctrine of the immortality of the soul by itself.

Without a body, the human spiritual soul is metaphysically deficient. It is a spirit that is meant to give life to a physical body and to exercise itself in a body. It gains knowledge through the exercise of reason from information obtained from the senses. This intelligence is oriented toward life in a body. That is why a complete restoration of the soul calls for a body in and through which the soul may express itself. A human soul differs from an angelic spirit in that the latter is created to know and express itself in a purely spiritual state of being.

For Paul, the resurrection of Christ was brought about by the Spirit of God, the life-giving power of the Creator. The designation of the risen body as a "spirit-body," as a body formed by the Spirit, is a further indication of the same idea. The mode of existence belonging to the risen Lord is determined by the Spirit *(pneuma)*, so that Paul can actually say "The Lord is in the

Spirit" (2 Cor 3:17). As a result of the dynamic unity between them, the Lord acts through the Spirit upon those who have been baptized in such a way that they are "in him" and he is "in them." In virtue of this, he, together with them, constitutes a unity that can be called "one body" (1 Cor 12:12–13) and "one spirit" (1 Cor 6:17).

It is not a question of either a soul immortal by nature and thus acting normally in its "separated" state, nor a soul necessarily tied to a body and condemned to "sleep" as long as the latter is dead. It is a question of a "spirit" placed in us by the indwelling of the Spirit of Christ (2 Cor 5:5), from which source we draw all the strength of a new, supernatural, mysterious, but real life.

What has been implicit in this reflection thus far now remains to be made explicit: Jesus did not rise from the dead for himself alone. Just as the first-fruits are only the first part of the harvest and not the whole, so too it is with his resurrection. It is not an isolated event; were that the understanding, we would not be talking about it here with reference to ourselves. Though it may be difficult for us to think of it in anything but individualistic terms, if we wish to remain faithful to the biblical testimony, we must not separate the destiny of the individual from that of the community—the Body of Christ—and of the entire created order. Paul's teaching on this is repeated and clear: we are crucified and buried with him (Rom 6:4–6); we live with him (6:8); we are heirs with him and are glorified with him (8:17); and we will be changed to become like his glorious body (Phil 3:21).

Such assertions are not without their implications for our present lives. To wit: the Spirit bestowed upon us is not dormant within us, but is already in this present time actually bringing about that inner transformation which is intended to lead up to the glory that lies in the future. We are being renewed constantly, and our corporeal dimension has to take part in this spiritual renewal. As we presently know them, our bodies cannot enter the new world and will have to be changed by Spirit. Will the final and definitive transformation happen at the end of time or immediately after death? Biblical scholar Pierre Benoit responds in these terms:

> To sum up, if according to the traditional faith we must believe that our bodies will rise at the end of the world…, at the same time we must acknowledge that we have no idea at all of what this end of our times corresponds with in the new and already present world in which the risen Christ lives. And since, in addition, we know that we are already united here below in the Holy Spirit with the body of the risen Christ, we are able to believe that directly after death we shall find in this uninterrupted union the source and means of our essential blessedness.[7]

Resurrection is a teaching about the meaning and fate of the human body. What God did for Jesus reveals what God plans to do for us. The doctrine of the resurrection says that the body itself is not a product, not a consumable. Though biodegradable, it is not disposable. Though broken, flawed, worn out, each human body continues to be precious to its designer. God does not plan to throw my body away like a banana peel or a polyvinyl chloride bottle. God plans to keep the whole thing, the whole me. Christians "teach" resurrection by devising ways of life that care for human bodies.[8]

Thus, a sound holistic spirituality recognizes the importance of proper and disciplined care for the body and its needs while cultivating union with God. In Christian understanding, we are rooted in our bodies. At birth, in our work and play, in our eating and love-making, in our living and dying, it is not simply that we *have* bodies, but that we *are* bodies.

The Role of the Body in Prayer

In spite of all these reference points in Christian faith, little positive attention has been given to the role of the body in prayer in the Western world. The irony is that the Eastern religions—which embrace either reincarnation (Hinduism) or karmic rebirth (Buddhism)—emphasize the enduring nature of the imperishable soul (Hinduism) or surviving karmic energy (Buddhism), but offer no salvation to the body; and yet they ascribe an important place to the body in their spiritual practices. Yoga, tai chi, aikido, breathing exercises, and walking meditation all come from Eastern religions.

Christians, on the other hand, with their high theological evaluation of the body, have little to offer by way of spiritual practices that work with and through the body. So it should come as no surprise that in this new era, when Westerners and Easterners are finding themselves living and working together and sharing notes with one another on the spiritual journey, that Christians would be learning from followers of Eastern religions and translating their own theological convictions into practice.

There is, I believe, a deep and subconscious recognition of wisdom and truth in the Christian psyche when encountering spiritual-life disciplines that take the body seriously. When that instinctive and intuitive response is confirmed in the body by a felt sense of rightness in performing these disciplines, then people integrate them into their life practices even before being able to articulate to themselves the connections between what they are doing and their faith. When someone comes along and gives explicit expression to the "fit" between the two, there is a moment of "Ah ha! Thank you for putting words on what I already knew in my body but had not yet fully grasped with my mind."

Westerners have been conditioned to think that prayer is mostly a mental activity, largely located in the brain. But prayer is not a bodiless experience done only in the head, nor only in the heart. It is an experience of the whole person. It is compatible with other activities such as looking at art, writing, walking, or swimming, as this poem written on one of my summer holidays witnesses to:

> Morning prayers are best said
> in the water, belly-up,
> facing the rising sun
> and immersed in the renewing
> feel of the font

with your ears submerged
so that everything you say
is magnified in the water
and flies straight up
to be heard by all the trees
and the mountains
and to be carried away on the wind
by the ravens and the gulls
for the rest of the world.

It was out of this kind of experience of prayer in and from the body that the Jewish mystic and rabbi Abraham Heschel said of his experience marching with Dr. Martin Luther King, Jr., in Alabama, "My feet were praying." The meaning in our heads becomes the meaning in our bodies. When we use our bodies with spiritual intent, both our bodies and the occasion become sacred. Sometimes these bodily actions accompany spoken prayers; sometimes they are prayers in and of themselves.[9]

When we pray, we should do so as a whole person and with those gestures and postures that seem most natural to us and are most meaningful for us. In corporate worship, we stand, sit, and kneel in uniform communal action. When we pray privately, we have the freedom to express ourselves in whatever way is helpful to us. There is a variety of ways that Christians express the dispositions of their hearts through their bodies. The psychology behind religious body language is the same as that expressed when a man says, "I kiss my wife because I love her; but kissing her also helps me love her." The various actions expressed through the body are meant to both incline and align the body toward and with the mind and heart. The Church's liturgical tradition seeks to engage physical participation in worship, to give everyone an active part. When we don't consciously play our parts and become passive spectators, the end result evokes an image not of God's chosen but of God's "frozen" people. What are some of the ways that Christians do engage their bodies in worship and prayer?

Roman Catholics and (some) Anglicans. Traditionally, a bow or genuflection (touching the right knee to the floor while keeping the upper body erect) is made upon entering and leaving a church. Both are a form of reverence and are made to the altar. The ritual for dedicating an altar in a new church is rich in its symbolism. The altar is liberally anointed with sacred oil and then the bishop spreads the oil over the entire surface as though anointing a body. The accompanying prayer refers to Christ being both the altar and the sacrifice. Thus, before beginning the Mass, the priest bows and kisses the altar. In Europe, particularly, genuflection was the way the altar was reverenced by all, though eventually Roman Catholics and high-church Anglicans came to prefer the distinction that if the Sacrament was on the altar or present in the sanctuary, a genuflection was used, and if it was not, a bow was employed.

The sign of the cross (also used by Eastern Christians) is another expression of religious body language. From early times this ritual action has enjoyed a widespread usage: crosses were traced with the thumb on the sick, with the hand over food at mealtimes, and on one's own forehead, chest, and shoulders at times of prayer. In an allusion to the sign of the cross being made with oil on the foreheads of the newly baptized, Martin Luther advised his followers, "Every morning get out of bed, cross yourself, and say, 'I am a baptized Christian.'" When bishops in the early Church could no longer be present at all baptisms, they would later visit those baptized and bless them with the sign of the cross; the bishops would bless the people as well in the name of the Trinity, making the sign of the cross over them collectively and giving us another use for it as a blessing "in the name of the Father and of the Son and of the Holy Spirit."

The sign of the cross has further been used in multiples, tracing it with the thumb on the forehead, lips, and chest before listening to the proclamation of the Gospel, signifying "May the word of the Lord be in my mind. May I speak it on my lips, and carry it always in my heart."

The sign of the cross is a bodily gesture of faith that parents teach to their children and that accompanies them from baptism to death. It pops up when one least expects it: in the middle of a basketball game with a free-throw shooter at the line; in an exam room before the students begin to write; in a car or plane before it begins to move; around a table with a family before meals; in the end zone when a player scores. Many begin or end their day with it. For Christians, it is the sign of redemption, God's "registered trademark." When those who use it cross themselves, they are telling themselves the most important thing they can say about themselves: that they are loved and saved at a great price. It is both a personal identity mark and a communal sign.

Another bodily gesture in worship is the kiss of peace, interpreted variously as a handshake or a kiss on one or both cheeks. It expresses a desire to be reconciled with one another, to be one in and at peace with all other members of Christ's Body, the Church.

Eastern Orthodox. In addition to the above, Eastern Christians employ one of the most pronounced expressions of prayer through the body to be found among the followers of Jesus. It is called a *metania,* from the Greek root *metanoia,* conversion. In the regular season of the church year, a *metania* consists of a deep bow from the waist with an accompanying gesture of the right hand coming down to touch the floor; when the one praying stands upright again, there is a fluid sweep up with the right hand and a signing of oneself with the sign of the cross. In Advent and Great Lent, the body is more fully engaged in the *metania:* one comes down onto the floor on one's knees and touches one's forehead to the floor, then rocks back onto one's feet and stands up, ending with the sign of the cross. This movement is generally done before an icon, and in Advent or Lent might be repeated one- or two-hundred times, inducing in the heart an attitude of repentance or humility.

The devotional and liturgical venerations of icons among Eastern Christians involves another instance of body language in prayer. An icon does not represent a saint as divine, but as participating in divine life, as one who has become a true icon or likeness of God. The faithful will kiss this image because they believe the grace of God rests upon it and in it. The Holy Spirit that filled the saints during their lives is believed to live on inexhaustibly, even after death, in their souls, in their mortal remains, in their writings, and in their holy images. Believers thus bow before the icons, kiss them, light candles before them, and pray.

Pentecostals. Pentecostals are known for their enthusiastic and expressive worship expressed in sound: singing in tongues, clapping or giving applause to the Lord, raising hands, and shouting loud "amens" and "alleluias." One of their standard forms of prayer is "concert prayer." It is a general time of prayer in which the entire congregation prays together loudly "in concert," in contrast to traditional modes of prayer which are led by one person, usually the pastor.

The expressive worship of Pentecostalism is often embraced by people who desire "heart religion" over more literary and intellectual forms of faith and worship. It appeals through its oral-gestural character and its participatory patterns. In Latin and African cultures in particular, spiritual dancing accompanies the singing, and this is by no means limited to the Pentecostals. One of my colleagues, Thomas Kane, CSP, has produced three award-winning videos featuring Catholic communities at worship in *The Dancing Church in Africa, The Dancing Church in the South Pacific,* and *Fiesta!*[10]

Prayer for healing, accompanied by the laying on of hands, is also common among charismatics and Pentecostals. Members of the community needing healing or counsel, or those about to be sent forth in service or to undertake positions of responsibility on the community's behalf, receive a blessing in the form of hands laid upon them in prayer.

Protestants. Most Protestant forms of worship include hymn-singing and prayer, scripture readings, a sermon, and sometimes Holy Communion. Engagement of the body is generally limited to standing, sitting, and bowing one's head in prayer.

The bowed head is one of the most familiar postures of prayer among Christians, accompanied by closed eyes and folded hands; this is the typical posture they use, for example, when giving thanks for the food they are about to eat at table. One of the inherent characteristics of ritual is that it is repetitive; it seeks to shape the heart and mind in a particular way—as here, in gratitude for all God's gifts. The definition of virtue is a good action that has become habitual.

Overall, the Christian pattern of engaging the body in prayer is not strong. There is a tendency to divorce spirit from matter and to regard the spirit as higher than the body. As Edwin Muir says of the Scottish Calvinism of his day in the poem "The Incarnate One," "The Word made flesh here is made word again."[11] We are inclined to translate the embodiment of God into an idea and turn away from our bodies, rather than locating the presence of God *in* our bodies.

The timidity and reluctance that many people feel around the Holy Thursday foot-washing ceremony exemplifies this. Why do we experience discomfort in this ritual? Is it because we have been conditioned to remove our bodies from the expression of our spiritual selves? In much of our secular culture, on the other hand, the body is idolized, particularly as it relates to the sexual. In both dichotomizing our bodies from our spirits and in idolizing physical comeliness by itself, we deny our sacredness as embodied spirits, made in God's image.

In the Gethsemani II Encounter in 2002, about twenty-five Buddhist and Catholic monastics came together for four days of dialogue at the Trappist monastery in Gethsemani, Kentucky. Each day the participants introduced one another to one of their sacred rituals. On one occasion, the Catholic participants read the passage from John's Gospel where Jesus washes the feet of his disciples in a gesture of humility and service, and then two of the Catholic participants proceeded to wash and dry the feet of those who sat in a circle. To express one's esteem and respect for the other in such concrete terms goes beyond the power of mere words. We think and say our love to each other and to God, but we often have difficulty expressing it through bodily gesture. The Buddhist monks clearly grasped that the act of foot-washing was a prayer performed by their counterparts with their hands.

The Witness of Scripture

Bodily expressions are associated with worship throughout scripture.[12] Sometimes expressiveness is a spontaneous reaction to what God has revealed and done. Miriam grabbed her tambourine and danced exuberantly with other women on the bank of the Red Sea (Exod 15:20). The Israelites bowed their heads before the Almighty when they heard how God was going to strike the firstborn sons of Egypt but spare their own children (Exod 12:17). Upon learning that the Lord promised to be with them in battle, the Levites "stood up to praise the LORD…with a very loud voice" (2 Chr 20:19). Job's response to losing his family and possessions was to fall to the ground and worship (Job 1:20). David danced joyfully before God as the ark of the covenant was being returned to Jerusalem (2 Sam 6:5, 16). Acts 3:8 describes the healed man as leaping and praising God.

These spontaneous reactions to particular events are fully consistent with the ways of praising God that are enjoined by the scriptures:

> Clap your hands, all you peoples! Shout to God with loud songs of joy! (Ps 47:1)

> Oh come, let us worship and bow down; let us kneel before the LORD, our Maker! (Ps 95:6)

> Let them praise his name with dancing, making melody to him, with tambourine and lyre! (Ps 149:3)

> Stand in awe of God! (Ps 22:23)

> I desire then that in every place the men should pray, lifting up holy hands. (1 Tim 2:8)

> The twenty-four elders fall down before the one who is seated on the throne and worship the one who lives forever and ever. (Rev 4:10)

Clapping, shouting, kneeling, dancing, playing instruments, standing in awe, lifting hands, falling down—all these actions are acceptable and appropriate in the worship of God. It is clear, however, that God desires more than just bodily gestures.

Lifting hands can signify a wide range of emotions and attitudes such as longing, expectation, thanksgiving, celebration, dependence. But if we mistreat the poor and abuse the unfortunate, God's response is like that expressed to the Israelites by the prophet Isaiah: "When you stretch out your hands, I will hide my eyes from you; even though you make many prayers, I will not listen, for your hands are full of blood" (Isa 1:15).

Similarly, God finds no pleasure in singing that is not accompanied by upright living: "Take away from me the noise of your songs; to the melody of your harps I will not listen. But let justice roll down like the waters and righteousness like an ever-flowing stream" (Amos 5:23–24). Even the simple act of standing can be offensive to God if unaccompanied by heart devotion. In Matthew 6:5, Jesus rebukes the hypocrites who "love to stand and pray in the synagogues and at the street corners, that they may be seen by others."

Some maintain that worship is a matter of the heart, not the body. But both are important. Engaging the body in true worship honors God. But if our expressions of worship on the outside do not line up with faith-filled devotion on the inside, there is no true worship. No amount of bodily expressiveness can make up for a divided or unrepentant heart.

Spiritual Exercises

As we look into our Christian treasure chest for accumulated wisdom relating to honoring the body, *The Spiritual*

Exercises written by Ignatius of Loyola in the sixteenth century offer one of the clearest and most influential expositions of what is called in Christian spirituality "the affirmative way."

Ignatian spirituality and mysticism find God in all things in order to love and serve God in all things. It is a mysticism of joy in the world that serves God in and through the world. It is an Easter spirituality that loves the earth because the trinitarian God creates, redeems, and loves the earth. Ignatius' mystical union with God did not incline him away from the senses and the world.

The Exercises are essentially meditations and contemplations on Christ's life, death, and resurrection to aid one in becoming free of all disordered loves, all inner and exterior compulsions, in order for the person to restore a right relationship with God and to seek to discover God's call in one's life. The power of this form of prayer comes from its ability to initiate the whole body-person in the Christian mysteries. The directives in the Exercises are meant to ensure that the retreatant fully utilizes his or her senses, emotions, passions, fantasies, memory, reason, intellect, heart, and will, in order to interiorize the material of the exercise.

Ignatius' "Application of the Senses" throughout the Exercises and especially in the meditations on hell, the Christmas story, and the passion underscore his extraordinary emphasis on the body. In praying with a biblical passage presenting Christ on the cross, for example, the retreatant is instructed to make a mental image of the place and to see, hear, taste, smell, and touch in imagination what is occurring in that particular event. Ignatius knew the importance of religious emotions. One is encouraged to give vent in prayer to spontaneous feelings and desires and to ask for tears, shame, sorrow, affectionate love, joy, gladness, peace, and tranquility.

The evidence of the body being moved was for Ignatius evidence that the spirit was being moved. In the consolation of tears, the body is acting in sympathetic vibration with the spirit; it shares in spiritual things when we weep, and with such tears, the body itself is being purified and sanctified. "My heart and my flesh sing for joy to the living God" (Ps 84:2). The whole self, body and spirit, is attuned to God who is its deepest joy.

In the Fifth Exercise for the First Week of *The Spiritual Exercises*, Ignatius provides some "Additional Directions" (no. 76) for the purpose of helping the retreatant to make the Exercises better and to find more surely that which is desired. Ignatius writes: "I will enter upon the meditation prostrate upon the ground, now lying face upwards, now seated, now standing, always being intent on seeking what I desire. If I find what I desire while kneeling, I will not seek to change my position; if prostrate, I will observe the same direction, etc."

Notice his clear recognition that the posture of the body is helpful in inciting the desired attitude in the heart. When one seeks to experience sorrow for one's sins, to kneel or lie prostrate before a crucifix is much more conducive to the grace sought than sitting in a comfortable recliner with feet up and arms folded.

Ignatius further recognizes the role of the body in prayer, emphasizing the centrality of movements within the heart during the prayer periods. In each prayer period in the Exercises, one begins with a prayer of dedication, then one imagines a scene appropriate to what is being meditated upon, then one asks for a grace. After this come several points for reflection. Following the reflection, there is what Ignatius calls the "colloquy."

In the colloquy, one pours out the heart as one would to a friend. Ignatius makes it very clear that what is important in the meditation is not what we figure out with the mind, not what insights we get, but how the Spirit moves us. Rational insight is clearly not enough. Ignatius wants those making the Exercises to open up to an affective relationship; he wants them to feel it in their bodies so that their movement toward God is not just on the rational level but on the level of the whole person.

Spouses know this from their own experience. If your relationship stayed forever at the level of the head, the exchange of ideas, it would never have engaged you enough as a whole person to the point that you were willing to move in with this person and share the same bed, bathroom, and bank account. The affective level of prayer is key. Among Hindus, *bhakti* yoga (seeking God through devotional expression) has many more adherents than *jnana* yoga (seeking God through study and reflection). And affectivity moves through the body, through the senses.

We have a body. The question is, how will it open us up to God in prayer? It is a springboard. All the practices of the spiritual life—praying with the scriptures, meditating, saying the rosary, journaling, focusing, spiritual reading—are only worth the time if they bring us to communicate heart-to-heart with God, if they coax forth from us a heartfelt response to what has been given.

The Spiritual Journey Goes
Through the Body

A few years ago, I made the forty-day version of the Spiritual Exercises of Ignatius, about which I have written more at length elsewhere.[13] During my retreat, in the second week of the Exercises, I had an experience that illustrates the difference that bringing one's body into the prayer can make. One morning as I awoke about 6:30, I sat up in bed and reached for my Bible on the lamp stand. My next assigned meditation was the passage from Luke's Gospel in which a woman, known in the town as a sinner, appears in the doorway while Jesus is dining at the home of Simon the Pharisee. On identifying Jesus, she proceeds to throw herself at his feet, bathing them with her tears and drying them with her hair (7:36–50).

I started to give the passage a slow reading, but got no more than three verses into it before experiencing an inclination to just put the Bible down and simply contemplate the woman's coming into the house with an alabaster jar of ointment, dropping to the floor behind Jesus at his feet, weeping, and then beginning to bathe his feet with her tears and dry them with her hair. In the previous week of the Exercises, we had meditated on the Creation story, including the Fall of Adam and Eve and our own perpetuation of their misguided choice. So the sins of my own life had been recently rehearsed and were ready at hand in my consciousness. As I pondered the scene in my imagination, I felt moved in my own heart, and there came yet another inclination:

to get out of bed and enter into the action of the gospel scene physically.

So I got down on the floor on my knees, took the icon of Christ from where it stood on the night table next to my bed, and placed it on the floor in front of me, as though I were going to anoint his feet. Entering more deeply into the meditation now due to the posture of my body, I found myself being given the gift of tears. Lest you envision a few random drops, let me simply indicate that it must have gone on for three-quarters of an hour. The closing verses brought me the deep peace of one who is both washed out emotionally and purified in spirit and body. "Her sins, which were many, have been forgiven, because of her great love....Then he said to her, 'Your sins are forgiven'...and, 'Your faith has saved you. Go in peace.'" I experienced those words as spoken to me, and it was one of the most powerful and penetrating prayer experiences of my life. I remained for a long time on the floor, filled with the kind of deep gratitude that is ready to give its life in return.

The gifts of tears and laughter are among the signs of empowered release. Tears do not necessarily mean sadness or depression. Tears can be a cleansing act of opening, an expression of gratitude and love pouring forth from the deep springs of inner life. Even when tears do come from grief, grieving openly and freely is a bodily sign of trust and release.

The reason that I share this story here is simply this: I am sure those purifying tears would never have come if I had entered into that meditation sitting upright in bed. It was what I did with my body in getting down on my knees that was the trigger. The posture of the body opened the door for what was in the heart and bid it come forth.

We have a body. Will we give it its due place in our spiritual lives?

Notes

1. Margaret Brennan, "Our Likeness to God," PMC: *The Practice of Ministry in Canada* (May, 1996), 25.

2. *The Revelations of Divine Love*, James Walsh, SJ, trans. (St. Meinrad, IN: Abbey Press, 1974), 63.

3. Stephanie Paulsell, *Honoring the Body* (New York: Jossey-Bass, 2002), 5, 34.

4. "Honoring the Body," in *Practicing Our Faith: A Way of Life for a Searching People,* Dorothy C. Bass, ed. (New York: Jossey-Bass, 1998), 19.

5. Brenda Peterson, *Nature and Other Mothers* (New York: Fawcett Books, 1995), 13–18.

6. Franz Mussner, as quoted in Joachim Gnilka, "Exegetical Understanding of the Resurrection of the Body," in *Immortality and Resurrection*, Pierre Benoit and Roland Murphy, ed., The New Concilium Series (New York: Herder and Herder, 1970), 140.

7. Pierre Benoit, "Resurrection: At the End of Time or Immediately After Death?" in *Immortality and Resurrection*, 114.

8. Marianne Sawicki, in the essay "Teaching as a Gift of Peace," quoted in Martin Marty's newsletter *Context* (March 15, 1991), 6.

9. Jon Sweeney, *Praying with Our Hands: 21 Practices of Embodied Prayer from the World's Spiritual Traditions* (Woodstock, VT: SkyLight Paths Publishing, 2000), 20.

10. Obtainable at www.paulistpress.com.

11. Edwin Muir, *Collected Poems* (London: Faber & Faber, 1984), 228.

12. I am indebted in this section to Bob Kauflin's online four-part article series, "Worship Matters: Bodily Expression and the Worship of God," at www.crosswalk.com.

13. Thomas Ryan, *Four Steps to Spiritual Freedom* (Mahwah, NJ: Paulist Press, 2003).

3.

The Body Language of Faith

Thomas Ryan

The spiritual life in general and prayer in particular cover a much broader range of human activity than what we do in church. Melted down to its essence, prayer is presence responding to Presence. Since the Divine Presence never leaves us, it is incumbent upon us to cultivate our awareness and responsiveness of heart to God's presence with and in us wherever we are and whatever we are doing. It could only have been this kind of more pervasive awareness of the God in whom "we live and move and have our being" that Paul had in mind when enjoining us to "pray in the Spirit at all times" (Eph 6:18) or to "give thanks in all circumstances" (1 Thess 5:18).

Thus our "body language" in our relationship with God is much richer and more multilayered than the posture of our body at worship. This broader body language includes fasting and feasting, exercise and rest, suffering and sexual intercourse, and forms of social engagement as expressed in corporal works of mercy. In reflecting on the diversity of this language, we see that our physical bodies qualify everything about us.

A doctor in a palliative care unit dropped a comment once that impressed upon me just how real the physical body is. "There are four kinds of suffering," he said. "Physical, emotional, spiritual, and social. And you can't effectively alleviate people's emotional, spiritual, or social pain until you have addressed their physical pain. Until there is physical relief, the person can't think or focus on anything else."

What are some of the ways in which our embodied being both inclines us toward and facilitates our relationship with God?

Feasting and Fasting

The neighborhood in which I live in midtown Manhattan exemplifies the bounty and variety of nourishment available to us in the Northern Hemisphere. When visitors come to town and express an inclination to dine out, I ask them what kind of food they have a yen for, and proceed to tick off the restaurants within a ten minute walk: Greek, Chinese, Thai, Italian, American, Spanish, Indian, French, Ethiopian, Swiss, and Mexican. And as good as the fare is dining out, many are the evenings when what is served at our own table would trump the competition. I live in a community of twenty-seven, a third of whom are in retirement and for whom the meals are principally prepared; the rest of us benefit by association.

The gathering of people around the table is part of what nourishes. An advantage of living in a large community is that there is always someone with whom to share both food and conversation. And if the truth be told, we spend more time relating to one another around the table than anywhere else. How wonderful that God opens us up to one another through the need of our bodies for nourishment! The variety of personalities and interests and involvements around the table responds to an even deeper hunger—for connectedness in relationship. The table is a place not just where bellies are filled but where relationships are forged, where friendships grow, and where hatchets are buried. A genuine feast is defined not merely in terms of food but in intellectual stimulation through conversation and in relational warmth.

In our community, what is put on the table is so consistently tasty and copious that the difference between a normal day and a genuine holiday feast is more in the tablecloth and napkin than in the food on the platter. But feasting every day takes the edge off the occasions that cry out for a feast. The body language of faith provides a place for voluntary abstention. It might mean limiting oneself to a single portion as an expression of "moderation in all things" (have you ever noticed that the third helping never tastes as good as the first?), or it might take the form of a weekly fast day to stay consciously in touch with deeper, inner hungers. One of the things a weekly fast day does is heighten one's appreciation for the presence and the taste of food on the other six days. It is a reward that makes being constantly sated pale by comparison.

Always when we voluntarily go without food, it is because something else is more important to us. It might be an early departure, a slim waistline, or a feeling of physical well-being. Fasting as an act of conscious relationship with God, however, has a different spin to it.

The value of any particular discipline in the spiritual life is in direct proportion to its ability to make us more aware of God as the deepest reality of our lives. In fasting as a religious act, we in effect say, "God, you are number one to me. You are more important to me than life itself, which food symbolizes for me. With this fast I want to send you that message and impress upon myself that you are at the center of life's meaning."

Yes, food is important. Yes, I need it. But all the needs of my life, if traced down to the deepest core, are rooted in my single greatest need: fulfillment from the hand of my Creator. Fasting is a concrete, decisive act that says, "You, Lord, are the still point in my turning world, and please don't ever let me forget it. For you I will upset my routine of three meals today because you are the God I worship, not my routine. For you I will give up meeting my friends for lunch today because, even though I need them and like them very much, the love and acceptance I need from them is only a reflection of the love and acceptance I need from you. For you I will live with these hunger pangs today and let them speak to me of my deepest hunger: 'Our hearts are restless, Lord, until they rest in you.'"

Meals are important in so many ways—as a social event, as a needed break from work, as nutrition. When we voluntarily forego food as part of our language with God, it takes on the meaning that we are willing to set aside all else in favor of seeking God. From time to time I can forget just which needs in my life are the most important, and my priorities can become all mixed up. Precisely because eating symbolizes that which is most important to us (life and growth), when we set food and drink aside to seek God, we're declaring that God is more important and essential a source of life and growth for us than anything else. It is essentially God's love that creates, sustains, and restores us at the core of our being.

And make no mistake about it: this is a *body* prayer par excellence. The very space created in the stomach is the incarnate symbol that we want to create more room in our hearts for this relationship. It is a prayer that is *felt* in the body through the course of the day. The value of fasting as a religious act lies in the faith and love of which it is the expression. The point at which our human freedom reaches its peak is when we, having experienced in our daily lives the abundant love of God for us, move freely and spontaneously to return God's love. It is not the hardship or sacrifice involved that is ennobling, but the motive to offer God a free response of love. Fasting has few equals in completely engaging one's embodied spirit in a day-long prayer.

What holds true for holistic spirituality in general holds true for fasting in particular: If it's good for my soul, it's good for my body; and if it's good for my body, it's good for my soul. What we know physiologically about the benefits of fasting can be integrated into our motivation. A fast day is an opportunity for the body to "clean house." When it is given a day off from its normal process of digestion, assimilation, and elimination, the body will use the occasion to cleanse itself of toxins, throw off old cells, and tend to a general refurbishing. When we drink only water or natural juices during a fast, the effect is much the same as when we wring out a dirty sponge. The liquids facilitate the flushing out of waste materials that keep us running at low-level performance, feeling sluggish, and being less in the mood to give God joyful praise for the gift of life and health. The manuals are in agreement: one should drink at least eight to ten glasses of water and/or juice on a fast day.

There is yet another dimension to feasting and fasting: solidarity. As St. Augustine reminds us, a fast undertaken at the urging of the Spirit of God will result in practical outreach: "Certainly you have deprived your body, but to whom did you give that which you deprived yourself? Fast, then, in such a way that when another has eaten in your place you may rejoice in the meal you have given."[1]

In reflecting on the story of Israel being sustained by manna in the desert, Stephanie Paulsell asks, "What would manna look like in our own day?"

It would look like food generously shared from hand to hand. It would look like communities that take responsibility for the well-being and nourishment of others....That is why table blessings so often hold together gratitude for God's sustenance and remembrance of those who hunger. For remembering the one should lead us to think of the other. Every time we sit down to a meal, we should remember two things: that life is sustained by God and that there are many, beloved by God, who do not have enough to eat. Gratitude and solidarity, practiced over and over, three times a day, ought to shape not only how we receive our nourishment but how we receive our neighbor as well.[2]

At the heart of the Judeo-Christian-Islamic way of relating to God is a triad of practices: prayer, fasting, and almsgiving (the sharing of one's possessions). Their interrelatedness cannot be stressed enough. Each is meant to be an aid to the others. Together they harmoniously relate us to God, to others, and to ourselves. The corollary to responding to God in a spirit of prayerfulness is responding to the need we see around us. The fast God has chosen is directly related to social responsibility:

> Is not this the fast that I choose:
>> to loose the bonds of injustice,
>> to undo the thongs of the yoke,
> to let the oppressed go free,
>> and to break every yoke?
> Is it not to share your bread with the hungry,
>> and bring the homeless poor into your house;
> when you see the naked, to cover them,
>> and not to hide yourself from your own kin?
>
>> (Isa 58:6–8)

Corporal Works of Mercy

The above verses from Isaiah find expression in another modality of Christian body language, traditionally known as the corporal works of mercy. They are to feed the hungry, give drink to the thirsty, shelter the homeless, visit the sick, clothe the naked, ransom the captive, and bury the dead.

The biblical source of these works is, in addition to Isaiah, the challenging teaching of Jesus that we encounter him in all who hunger or thirst, in all who are homeless or sick, in all who are naked or in prison. When we respond to their needs, it is his needs that we give to; when we turn away from them, it is from him that we turn (Matt 25:31–46).

While in India in the early nineties, I heard the Benedictine pioneer in interfaith dialogue, Fr. Bede Griffith, speak about the Christian-Hindu dialogue in his local area. He recounted how, at the end of one of their sessions, he invited the Hindu participants to come to his ashram at any time to join the Christians in meditation. One of the Hindu participants reacted with surprise: "Really? You mean you Christians meditate? I thought you just ran hospitals and schools and social agencies!"

Why have the corporal works of mercy come to character- ize Christian engagement with the world in the form of hospi- tals, shelters, soup kitchens, food pantries, and clothing distribution centers? As Fr. Ron Rolheiser so aptly explains, it is due to the ongoing nature of the incarnation in Christian under- standing.

The incarnation is not a thirty-three year experiment by God in history, a one-shot, physical incursion into our lives. The incarnation began with Jesus and it has never stopped. The ascension of Jesus did not end, nor fundamentally change, the incarnation. God's physical body is still among us. God is still present, as physical and as real today, as God was in the historical Jesus. God still has skin, human skin, and physically walks on this earth just as Jesus did. In a certain manner of speaking, it is true to say that, at the ascension, the physical body of Jesus left this earth, but the body of Christ did not. God's incarnational presence among us continues as before.[3]

In other words, what Christ did in and for the world of his day through his physical presence, the community does in and for the world today. We are now God's physical hands, feet, mouth, and heart in our local context. We mediate Christ to the little space under our feet and within our reach. The Grail Prayer with which I begin each new day expresses it in these words:

> Lord Jesus, I give you my hands to do your work.
> I give you my feet to go your way.
> I give you my eyes to see as you do.
> I give you my tongue to speak your words.
> I give you my mind, Lord, that you may think in me.
> I give you my spirit, that you may pray in me.

Most of all, I give you my heart, Lord,
That you may love in me your Father and all humankind.
I give you my whole self, so that it is you, Lord Jesus,
Who lives and works and prays in me.

Rolheiser goes on to reflect how the New Testament's reference to the "Body of Christ" means three things:

> *Jesus*, the historical person who walked this earth for thirty-three years; the *Eucharist*, which is also the physical presence of God among us; and the *body of believers*, which is also the real presence. To say the word "Christ" is to refer, at one and the same time, to Jesus, the Eucharist, and the community of faith.
>
> We are the Body of Christ. This is not an exaggeration, nor a metaphor. To say that the body of believers *is* the Body of Christ is not to say something that scripture does not. Scripture, and Paul in particular, never tells us that the body of believers *replaces* Christ's body, nor that it *represents* Christ's body, nor even that it is Christ's *mystical* body. It says simply: "We *are* Christ's body."[4]

The most comprehensive theological forum in Christendom, the 120-member Faith and Order Commission of the World Council of Churches, spoke with one voice in testifying to Christian faith in the reality of Christ's presence in the Eucharist:

...the eucharistic meal is the sacrament of the body and blood of Christ, the sacrament of his real presence....But Christ's mode of presence in the eucharist is unique. Jesus said over the bread and wine of the eucharist: "This is my body...this is my blood...." What Christ declared is true, and this truth is fulfilled every time the eucharist is celebrated. The Church confesses Christ's real, living and active presence in the eucharist.[5]

The Faith and Order Commission members, representing virtually all the major church traditions, then went on to draw out the implications of this for Christian living, and in so doing, underlined the conviction of faith that the body of believers, like the Eucharist, is the Body of Christ in an organic, real way:

The eucharistic communion with Christ who nourishes the life of the Church is at the same time communion within the body of Christ which is the Church. The sharing in the one bread and the common cup in a given place demonstrates and effects the oneness of the sharers with Christ and with their fellow sharers in all times and places....

The eucharistic celebration demands reconciliation and sharing among all those regarded as brothers and sisters in the one family of God and is a constant challenge in the search for appropriate relationships in social, economic and political life (Matt.

5:23f; I Cor. 10:16f; I Cor. 11:20–22; Gal. 3:28). All kinds of injustice, racism, separation and lack of freedom are radically challenged when we share in the body and blood of Christ….As participants in the eucharist, therefore, we prove inconsistent if we are not actively participating in this ongoing restoration of the world's situation and the human condition.[6]

The Risen One who calls us to the table has wounds in his body. They prevent us from forgetting those who still suffer. They remind us that the space around the table can hold together both suffering and healing, both despair and hope, both death and resurrection.

When a Doctor of the Law asked Jesus, "Master, which commandment in the law is the greatest?" Jesus responded by bringing together Deuteronomy 6:5 (love of God) and an obscure text that had never before been linked with it, Leviticus 19:18 (love of neighbor): "'You shall love the Lord your God with all your heart, and with all your soul, and with all your mind'….And a second is like it: 'You shall love your neighbor as yourself.' On these two commandments hang all the law and the prophets" (Matt 22:34–40). Love of neighbor is not the second commandment, subordinate to the first; it is a second command that is "like," that is, similar in character and equal in importance to, the first. The Old Testament, both in its legal codes and in its prophetic exhortations, abounds in prescriptions that urge concern for one's fellow human beings and prohibit the exploitation of the powerless. But interhuman concern here is always a secondary attitude that follows from a prior religious experience or a primary commitment to God. With Jesus the ethical attitude becomes, as it were, an integral part of the religious experience itself, for to experience God as "Father" is to experience the neighbor as "brother" and "sister." The horizontal is thus inseparably welded into the vertical, and love of neighbor is brought onto a level with love of God.[7]

Time and again Jesus makes it clear that love of God and love of neighbor are not separate realities or dimensions of life, but two sides of the same coin. They're so closely related, in fact, that the New Testament uses the same Greek word—*koinonia*—to describe them both. The point is that the deeper our relationships with one another, the deeper our relationship will be with Jesus himself. What an amazing thought: We can participate in the life of Christ only to the degree that we are in solidarity and communion of life with one another.

This underlying faith-vision of the Body of Christ is what makes the corporal works of mercy part of the body language of Christian living. It is because we see Jesus as *embodied* in the other that we increasingly move toward the *corporal* works of mercy. When we honor the bodies of others, we honor him. And because the biblical tradition understands the human person to be a *living body* rather than a *soul* temporarily and somewhat accidentally inhabiting a body, it gives a special importance to these corporal works of mercy. In fact, it is precisely such expressions of social concern that are proposed most frequently and most explicitly by Jesus and his followers as the most authentic criteria of genuine Christian love (Matt 20:31–46; 1 John 3:17–19; Jas 2–7, 14–17).[8]

Nor does the notion of solidarity end there. In speaking of the resurrection, the apostle Paul emphasizes the solidarity between the destiny of the individual and that of the entire created order (Rom 8:18–25). The first man and woman were created in the divine image, at one with themselves and with their environment. After the Fall, however, they are subject to compulsions, ashamed of their nakedness, divided within themselves, under the power of death, and alienated from nature and the animal world. Just as the enslavement of the first humans through sin involved the whole created order, so the creation of the new humanity, a new being in Christ, carries with it the entire cosmos, which meanwhile groans in travail, finding only in humankind an articulation of its hope for freedom from decay.[9]

Hence it must be stressed that the resurrection of the dead is *not* simply a guarantee of personal survival after death. If we wish to remain faithful to the biblical testimony, we must not separate the destiny of the individual from that of the community—the Body of Christ—and of the entire created order. The resurrection of the body expresses primarily and essentially the destiny of the new community, the eucharistic body, the body of the risen Christ, which is the nucleus of a worldwide community.[10]

Sexual Expression of Love

The central assertion of the Genesis story is that all life comes forth from the mystery of God. In that story, the difference between Adam and Eve and all the other creatures is shown above all by the fact that only *their* creation results from a deliberate decision on God's part to establish a specific bond with the Creator: "Let us make humankind in our image, according to our likeness....So God created humankind...male and female..." (Gen 1:26, 27).

In a series of homilies between 1979–1984, Pope John Paul II developed a theology of the body relative to the Church's teaching on love, sex, and marriage. Reflecting on these verses from Genesis, he notes how God created us in God's own image, not as generic human beings, but specifically as male and female. This means that our sexual complementarity, the very construction of our bodies, reveals something significant about God. The body reveals a profound truth: that we are created for relationship, for interpersonal union. The male and female bodies are designed for union with each other. Along with this capacity we discover a built-in attraction and fascination with one another. Adam recognized in Eve a person to whom he could give himself completely, someone who could receive and reciprocate his gift to form a union of love. This deep personal union is enacted in their very bodies through sexual union. So amazingly powerful and life-giving is this union that it can even result in the existence of another person![11]

In short, the language of the body is that we are made for communion, for interpersonal union in which we freely give ourselves to another in love. This call to communion is written into our very embodiment as male and female. The unique capacity of the body to express self-giving love is what John Paul II calls "the nuptial meaning of the body." "I am a gift!" declares the human body. "I have the capacity to give myself freely to another person in an intimate union of love." That meaning is not limited to those joined in marriage. All men and women—including the single, the consecrated celibates, and the widowed—live out this nuptial meaning by being a gift to others in various ways. Our bodily natures were created to transfer into the visible reality of the world the mystery hidden since time immemorial in God: *we were made for communion*. When we live in self-giving love in families, in the community of the Church, in communities of consecrated life, in circles of friends and colleagues, we are reflecting the inner dynamic of God's own life as a communion of Persons pouring themselves out in love for one another.[12]

Christianity came into existence in the Greco-Roman world at a time when the basic worldview perceived the material world and the human body as restraints, chains binding the freedom of the human spirit. This cast sexuality in a negative light as a burden warranting justification in terms of continuing the family, the tribe, the clan. This combination of philosophical pessimism and the economic approach to reproduction shaped the matrix in which Christian ethicists thought about sex for most of the Church's history. It has taken us two thousand years to break away from the Platonic, dualistic worldview and to get it clear that sex is not something evil of which to be ashamed.

The belief that our bodies are made in the image of God led the Jewish tradition to affirm the sacredness of the human body, including the holiness of the genitals. The genitals are associated with the genesis of all life in God. In Jewish mystical practice the covering of the phallus with foreskin symbolized humanity's tendency to cover over or to forget that our origins are in the loins of God. Thus the foreskin of the male child is cut away from the phallus, "and it shall be a sign of the covenant between me and you" (Gen 17:11). The Book of Deuteronomy uses feminine imagery when it says, "You forgot the God who gave you birth" (32:18). Our genitals are to remind us that ultimately our life is from God.[13]

Reflecting on Christianity's struggle to fashion a positive understanding of sexuality commensurate with its theology of the incarnation, J. Philip Newell says, "At different points in Christian history, if there had been a religious ritual in relation to the male genitals, it might well have taken the form not of circumcision, but of emasculation. Again and again the Christian tradition has failed to make a profound connection between our spirituality and our humanity, between the mystery of God on the one hand, and the mystery of the human body on the other."[14]

As we become genuinely more holistic in our spirituality, affirming all the dimensions of our being, sexual feelings often intensify. Many think that sexuality will go away or at least become quieter as we grow spiritually. But the contrary is true, and it only makes sense: as we grow into deeper communion with the Source of all life and love and creative energy, the God of the incarnation, we begin to experience even more eros in our encounter with others and the world. We begin to experience sexual energy in a new way, as a sacred, generative force.

The sexual dimension of our beings and relationships can lead us into a sense of the holy at levels deeper than conscious understanding. Oftentimes people seem to be praying to have their sexuality removed so they won't have to struggle with it anymore. That is a denial of a powerful, creative energy that connects us to one another. We *should* be struggling with it, like Jacob with the angel, for it is a messenger from God. An eighteenth-century rabbi in the Jewish mystical tradition recounted how he came to see pleasure and holiness not as opposed to each other but as one:

> I once heard a chaste man bemoaning the fact that sexual union is inherently pleasurable. He preferred that there be no physical pleasure at all, so that he could unite with his wife solely to fulfill the command of the Creator: "Be fruitful and multiply."...I took this to mean that one should sanctify one's thought by eliminating any intention of feeling physical pleasure. One should bemoan the fact that pleasurable sensation is inherent to the act. If only it were not so! Sometime later, God favored me with a gift of grace, granting me understanding of the essence of sexual holiness. The holiness derives precisely from feeling the pleasure. This secret is wondrous, deep, and awesome.[15]

This "wondrous secret" did not lead to a lawless self-indulgence or promiscuity in the Jewish mystical kabbalistic tradition. There were strict boundaries to marital relationship, precisely because sexual union was sacred. But sexual union also needs to be named as a sacred pleasure rather than left strangely unmentioned in our family lives. Amid all the talk of self-donation and mutuality, why is it so hard to say, "plus, it feels good!"? It is our inhibitions around naming genital pleasure as both good and of God, says Newell, that have led to a tendency to spiritualize that greatest of love poems, The Song of Songs. In it the bridegroom speaks of being "drunk with love" (5:14) and the bride says, "Let my beloved come to his garden, and eat its choicest fruit" (4:16).

> The bride describes the beloved knocking at her door, desiring to enter. He "thrusts his hand into the open-ing," she says, "and my inmost being yearned for him. I arose to open to my beloved, and my hands dripped with myrrh, my fingers with liquid myrrh, upon the handles of the bolt. I opened to my beloved." Such a passage speaks of the pleasure of the passion in our loins in sensuous and full-blooded ways. The sap of life and the moisture of sexual energy are celebrated in the poem. Its depths are achieved precisely because the spiritual and the physical are not torn apart but are inseparably interwoven. When we regard our body or the body of another simply as flesh we cheapen the sexuality of our being and lose sight of the spiritual depths that are within us. Pleasure is greatest precisely when we touch the spiritual dimen-sion that is within the physicalness of our bodies.[16]

For the churches that speak of marriage as sacrament, the clear understanding is that the conjugal union of two in love is a means of grace—that is to say, a source of growth in the divine life—for each. The sexual expression of love is considered so central to the way the spouses mediate this divine energy to one another that if either is unwilling or unable to consummate the relationship in physical, genital love-making, it is considered grounds for invalidating the marriage. One would have to say that the body language is considered critical to the vitality of the relationship and recognized as a synergistic meeting place between the human and the divine.

But there is no discourse on body language where suffering is not part of the grammar. A theology of the body must also recognize the ways in which human sexual existence is difficult. Lest we lose ourselves in flights of lyricism on the pleasures of sexual expression, let us admit how arduous and ambiguous a process it is for any of us to become sexually healthy and well-balanced; how unstable and shifting are the patterns of our sexual identity; how unpredictable and vagrant are our desire and craving, as well as our revulsion and resistance. Let us recognize how much the stresses of our lives bear upon our sexual expression. And let us honestly acknowledge that, for many who are married, the pleasure and comfort of sexual love are most needed precisely when least available due to sickness, anxiety, separation, divorce, and death. Our tendency is to speak only of the "original solitude" that finds its cure in marriage, and not of the "continuing solitude" of those both married and single whose vocation is not celibacy but whose erotic desires find no legitimate or sanctified expression.[17]

Exercise and Rest

Many of the retreats I lead work with themes in holistic spirituality in which it is not unusual for the topic of exercise to surface. When I ask people why they exercise, these are some of the reasons they give:

Self-image	Get in touch with my body
Quality of life	Physical fitness
Sublimate sexual energy	Maintain mental alertness
Lose weight	Work with my limits
Emotional equilibrium	Generate energy
Connect with friends	Divert stress
Aid digestion	Response to mental fatigue
Feel better	Enjoyment
Resiliency of health	Contemplative space
Release from study	Allows me to eat more
	Makes me better for others

This list, by no means exhaustive, testifies that exercise goes far beyond recreation and pleasant diversion. Anything that does all or even a *few* of these things for us—blow off angry steam, soothe jangled nerves, push along bulky food, teach us to respect and cooperate with others, smile at the limits with which our bodies are laden—should be honored for its direct contribution to our spiritual growth.

Spiritual growth? Yes, spiritual growth. Let us say it again: the spiritual life extends not only to the concerns of the soul, but to the life of the whole human person. The whole takes first place, rather than the parts. The human person is not a soul and a body, but inspirited flesh, an animated body. One *is* one's body and *is* one's soul at one and the same time. Holistic spirituality challenges us to integrate all aspects of our lives into our relationship with God.

Why is it that many more secular groups than church communities promote a healthy life, build friendship networks, generate significant amounts of funds, and contribute to worthy causes through a variety of organized exercise events like road races, bike tours, and walkathons? Why do members of the Church, whose teaching on the human body via the incarnation and resurrection is both profound and exciting, take so few initiatives in programs that draw out the practical consequences of what is at the heart of their theology?

We arrive at wholeness and holiness by using to the full the stuff of human experience, not by denying it or seeing it outside the pale of faith. The human qualities underlying fitness activities are the same as those underlying certain devotional practices: discipline, dedication, attention, and perseverance, to cite just a few. These are the human virtues that get us out of bed before the sun is fully up to meditate or to go for a jog. The virtue is the same; only the application is different. Just as strengthening these virtues in devotional practices can make their application easier in fitness activities, so can various forms of exercise cultivate virtues needed for meeting the challenges of the inner life of the spirit.

Through skiing, rock climbing, or white-water canoeing, one learns how to deal with and overcome fear and anxiety. Through running, swimming, or rowing long distances, one develops endurance and willpower and learns to deal with boredom. Through golf, one can practice intense concentration and subtle control. Team sports teach the values of cooperation and interdependence. In general, exercise develops self-awareness and self-control, knowledge of our limits, determination to succeed. It sets in motion and hones faculties critical to the spiritual life: attention, observation, analysis, judgment, evaluation.

Exercise can thus be both prayerful and ethically instructive, helping us to see the world more sharply and breathe the air more deeply. Any regular pattern of exercise that breeds affection for the embodied self, mocking it gently while urging it on, cultivates a spirit of human solidarity and compassion. When one has "been there," in however humble a fashion, one can more vigorously applaud the ballerina and the ball-carrier, the master of yoga and the mistress of natural childbirth. When one has "been there," fewer things human are foreign, and all things human are more precious. Jesus the carpenter and Jesus the poet more readily coincide.

The more attuned we become to the flesh God embraced and in which God dwells, exulting in its harmony, strength, and flexibility, learning how to bear its tensions and sufferings gracefully, the more we glorify its Creator, the One who also chose to call it "home." Being "spiritual" is not essentially a question of religious doctrines but of being very alive, very tuned-in and aware of the presence and movement of God's Spirit in creation, in relationships, and within our own bodies, hearts, and lives. It is primarily a question of refining our inner and outer senses to the presence of the Holy, daily in our midst.

Recently after giving some talks in Colorado, I went for a day's skiing in the Rockies. The friend I was with developed some health problems and never did get on the hill. He felt bad that I was left to ski alone, but I assured him that I never feel alone. I have a particular way of praying when I ski, especially when I am skiing by myself. I stop at the top of the run and allow some loved one to come to mind. I think of his or her needs and dedicate the descent as a prayer that he or she will be given what is needed that day. I lift up the exhilaration and the joy, the rhythm and the straining muscles, the accelerated heartbeat and the quickened breath, as an offering for my friend, a prayer written in the language of my body. And by the end of the afternoon, I feel like I have been on a retreat day, free-spiriting about the mountain, carving intercessions of love in the snow with my skis, the presence of many dear ones held close in my heart.

Rafting the Grand Canyon and climbing a mountain with family and friends have only confirmed for me that when the total involvement of the body and senses come together, the door opens for those quality moments the culture calls "mystical." Such moments will only surprise those who see the world without benefit of an incarnational spirituality. We should expect to find some pleasure waiting for us when we bring ourselves to exercise.

The counterpoint to exercise is rest. The two belong together. But without exertion, rest is inertia, laziness. And work without rest is slavery to either compulsion or economic necessity, but slavery.

In yoga, the "relax" pose consists of lying on the floor on one's back, palms up and feet turned out. For activity-driven citizens of our contemporary society, it is the hardest pose, more difficult in its own way than balancing on one leg or standing on one's head. Effort comes more naturally to most of us than non-effort. We can do almost anything with material space: fill it, change it, paint it, cover it, reinforce it, tear it down. But put us in front of an hour of uncharted, unprogrammed time, and we go catatonic or become spastic. Creative nondoing, genuine Sabbath time, is the greatest challenge of all. But it too is part of the body language of faith.

Inspiration from Other World Religions

Interreligious dialogue is both a gift and a task of our times. A corollary to believing that the Spirit of God has been active from the beginning of time among all peoples and cultures is that we must approach them with respect for their spiritual traditions to see what we can learn from them about pathways to God. In that spirit, I offer here some observations that have struck me in my encounters with people of other living faiths relative to their practices and understandings about the body.

Judaism

In the philosophy of Plato, the soul is a pure spiritual principle, distinct from the body and immortal. In Aristotelian philosophy, the soul is united with the body as a form united to matter; its spirituality and its immortality are less evident. The Semitic thinking of the Bible contributes a very different perspective. The Hebrew scriptures have no special word for the body. The whole person is "flesh" (basar), but also "soul" (nefes, i.e., life). The concept nefes can be signified by no single word in modern languages. We can only seek the meaning and describe it: the human person in his or her totality is a nefes, a psycho-physical totality.

We have already seen, in the above reflection on sexuality, the Jewish mystical tradition's affirmation of the whole of the human body. This unity surfaces repeatedly in Jewish life. "The Eighteen Blessings" within the daily cycle of prayers specifically requires bowing as part of the recitation. "The Eighteen" is also known as the *Amidah* ("standing") because the worshipper stands while reciting it. At the beginning of the *Amidah*, the one praying takes three steps forward, signaling entrance into God's presence, and at the end, three steps backward, to take one's leave. At the point in the blessings where God is praised, the worshipper acknowledges God's sovereignty and indicates submission by bowing, bending at the knees, then straightening, and gently bending from the waist. Some also employ the physical action of swaying back and forth while reciting the Word of God (*haga*). This movement, called *shuckling* from the Yiddish, suggests the action of the whole person coming under the spell of God through recitation of God's Word. "Let the words of my mouth and the meditation of my heart be acceptable to you, O LORD" (Ps 19:14).

Kabbalah (receiving) was a tradition of Jewish mysticism that emerged in medieval Europe. It taught a "receiving" of ancient wisdom both from the past and from deep within the human spirit. Kabbalistic tradition found a sacred text in the human body, seeing it as a microcosm of the sacred macrocosm of creation. There are parallels, for example, between the Jewish understanding of *sefirot* and the Eastern understanding of *chakras*, which are like energy centers in the human body. In the Jewish tradition, various points in our anatomy represent aspects of our living that are neglected or forgotten and need to be recovered.

> The crown of the head represents the mystery of our being. What cannot be said about us is always greater than anything that can be said. The forehead is identified with the wisdom of the divine image within us, a way of seeing that is deeper than outward sight. The arms are associated with strength; the left arm with power and the right arm with love. Do we know the strength that is within us, the strength for justice and the strength for love? The heart represents the beauty at the center of our being, a beauty that is deeper than the ugliness of what we have done or become in our lives. The genitals are associated with creativity and our God-given capacity to bring into being what has never been before. The legs are identified with a glory and eternity that are like the pillars of life. If they were to be removed, the temple of the universe itself would collapse. And the soles of our feet represent presence.

What does it mean to be a person of presence, to be present to others and to oneself in love?[18]

Shining through the material world is the spiritual world that upholds and enlivens it. Hidden in the mystery of our own bodies and the body of all creation is the Unseeable One. The way we treat the body of creation is, in the end, the way we treat the body of humanity. If we increasingly cut ourselves off from the glory that is in the earth and in one another, we will come to live as if the glory were not there. The less we allow ourselves to be touched by that glory, the less we will believe that glory is the foundation of life.

Islam

Islam teaches that all life is essentially a unity because it proceeds from the Divine Oneness of God. It offers a program of life that seeks complete coordination of the spiritual and the material aspects of human life. In the teachings of Islam, the coexistence and actual inseparability of both these aspects is insisted upon as the natural basis of life.

An illustration of this attitude is seen in the pilgrim's ceremony of walking around the *Ka'bah* or black stone in Mecca during the *hajj* or annual pilgrimage. Everyone who enters the Holy City must go seven times around the *Ka'bah*, which symbolizes the Oneness of God. The bodily movement of the pilgrims represents the activity of human life. The ritual implies that not only the pilgrim's devotional thoughts but also his or her practical life with all its actions and endeavors must have the idea of God at their center.

Most religions have daily prayer rituals, but Muslim daily prayer *(salat)* has no equal in the way that it integrates the body, mind, and spirit, illustrating the belief that we are to approach God through the sum total of the faculties God has bestowed upon us. "The Prayer," practiced around the world five times each day—dawn, midmorning, noon, midafternoon, and dusk—was taught to Muhammad by angels as a reflection of their constant adoration of God. It is not necessary to find a mosque, although Muslim men are enjoined to pray together there on Friday; one's body is the true mosque, and is to be daily used to honor and worship God. The prayer mat is to provide a clean space.

Before prayer come the ablutions. Eliminating minor ritual impurities involves removing shoes, washing hands, forearms, face, and feet, and sprinkling some water on one's head. Each of the five prayer periods have different units of prayer prostrations. Certain ones are necessary to fulfill the obligation of prayer. In praying together, straight lines are important for prayer needs to be aesthetically becoming and as much in unison as possible. In North America, Muslims face eastward to orient themselves to Mecca. The niche in the wall of the mosque, called a *qibla*, indicates the direction to face.

In the sequence of physical movements, one begins by bringing one's hands to the ears as a way of focusing on God while one says, *"Alahu akbar"* ("Allah is the greatest"). Then one folds the arms over the abdomen with the right hand grasping the left wrist, followed by a bow at the waist with the hands coming to rest just above knees (standing), saying three times, "Praise be to my Lord, the great One." Then one comes down onto the knees, touching the forehead and nose to the ground and saying, "Come to authentic living—Praise to my most high Lord." One then comes back to a sitting position with the tailbone on the heels, followed by another prostration of head to floor, before coming into a standing position, and then beginning the process all over again. The seven points of the body touching the ground during the prostrations—the feet, knees, hands, and face—are the seven limbs that the Prophet Muhammad pressed to the ground during his prayers. The number of prostrations are different depending on which prayer period of the day it is. At the end, the one praying looks to the right in recognition of the angel recording good deeds, and then to the left at the angel recording bad deeds, saying "Peace" to both. This last gesture is sometimes interpreted as acknowledging those with whom one is praying.

The body language of fasting also finds clear expression in Islam as one of the "five pillars" on which Islam is founded. During the lunar month of Ramadan each year, Muslims fast every day from dawn till sunset. During this time they do not eat, drink, smoke, or engage in sexual intercourse. The spirit of the fast extends as well to abstention from all evil thoughts, actions, and words. The emphasis is placed upon obedience to God, spiritual purification, charity to the poor, and the bonds of the Islamic community.

Buddhism

In *The Heart of Buddhist Meditation*, the largest section of the four foundations of mindfulness is on mindfulness of the body.[19] There are instructions in the *sutras* (basic Buddhist scriptures) on how to dress, eat, use the toilet, and so forth. Buddhists too employ a five-point prostration (feet-knees-arms-hands-head) as an integral part of their spiritual practice, and employ a bow for various occasions. For example, they bow three times when entering a room with a shrine in it, and three times when leaving the room. Monks bow to the abbot, and juniors to seniors, as a gesture of deference and respect. Another physical gesture, routinely used as an informal greeting or in approaching a teacher to ask for something, is the *anjalá*, with the palms together at the chest. Circumambulation is mentioned many times in the sutras. When people left the presence of the Buddha, they walked around him three times with their right shoulder (dexterous vs. sinister) toward him.

Bows in Zen Buddhism are usually done in sets of one, three, or one hundred and eight. In a full prostration, one begins by standing with the hands together at chest level, fingers pointed upward *(hapchang)*, as in a standing bow. The knees are dropped to the mat and the hands are placed, palms down, on the mat, with the left foot being laid on top of the right foot. As one leans forward to place the forehead on the mat and lowers the torso to the ground, the palms of the hands are turned upward, open to the sky. The feet are then flexed, and one rocks backward onto the heels and uses the legs to come back up into standing, with the hands again in *hapchang*. The objective is to achieve stillness of mind by paying attention to the motion; a mantra, coordinated with the movements, is also used for this purpose. The bowing is understood as little nudges urging one to wake up. As Andi Young, a practitioner of Korean Zen, says:

> When we put our hands out in front of us, our forehead down and our palms up, we are giving ourselves a physical example of how to train our minds: to put down our ego, and to open ourselves to the truth of our experience. When we show respect to the teacher and the Buddha in the meditation hall with our bows and our prostrations, we are also showing respect to ourselves and to our own ability to attain enlightenment. We are the Buddha; we're just too busy and confused, with all our emotions and thoughts going a million miles an hour, to find our own Buddha-nature. So we bow to the teacher and the Buddha to show that we respect and will cultivate our own Buddha-nature.[20]

Buddhist meditation practice has also given us the walking meditation. One of the Buddhist Gethsemani II participants, Venerable Heng Sure, abbot of the Berkeley Buddhist monastery, told me about his two-year-nine-month pilgrimage for world peace. He went from South Los Angeles to Ukaya, a one-hour drive north of San Francisco, journeying by making three steps and a prostration, three steps and a prostration, and so on. He covered a half-mile per day. I asked him how the experience would have been different just walking, without the prostrations. He spoke of how bowing cultivates humility and faith;

he also spoke of "conforming the mind to the good action of the body by giving it a positive content" through the practice of inner visualization, for example, seeing himself, in his imagination, bowing to the Buddha. There was also a penitential aspect to his pilgrimage and prostrations. He had told a lot of lies, he said, before entering the monastery; to amend for that, he kept silent the whole time, and his prostrations expressed his sense of repentance. An Orthodox Christian monk, accustomed to making hundreds of *metanias* before an icon during Lent, would understand exactly what he was talking about.

In the most common representation of the Buddha, he sits smilingly with eyes nearly closed as a sign that he has discovered the truth within himself. That posture in itself communicates the meaning of the Buddha: one who is enlightened. Buddhist meditation techniques use the body to master control of the mind. These techniques include focusing the mind on the sensation of breathing out and breathing in, and mental noting of sensations that arise in the body. These methods proceed from the body in order to bring the mind to one-pointed focus. The body is thus accorded an important role in the disciplines of the spiritual life.

Hinduism

In Hinduism, there are four yogas or disciplines that comprise the four paths to enlightenment (discerning the true nature of reality). *Jnana yoga* marshals the powers of the intellect to cut through the veils of illusion. *Bhakti yoga* directs one's love toward God through various devotional practices. *Karma yoga* is practiced through selfless service to others. *Raja yoga* is the path that leads to union with God through methods of concentration, control of the mind and senses, ending in meditation. Included in *raja yoga* is *hatha yoga*, which was designed to help one sit more quietly in one's body and with a more focused mind in meditation.

Pantajali, who lived somewhere between 500–200 BCE, was the first to offer a codification of yoga. In his *Yoga Sutras*, he described the ways of overcoming the obstacles to spiritual development in the form of afflictions of the body and fluctuations of the mind. The purpose of hatha yoga, he said, was to still the thought waves of the mind. The *asanas* or postures of hatha yoga are only correctly practiced if they fulfill the central purpose of stilling the mind.

On the surface, hatha yoga looks like no more than a collection of stretching exercises and breathing techniques. But when they are performed slowly with grace and control, as a type of meditation rather than as a form of calisthenics, they bring one ultimately to a state of inner quiet. The result is an experience of equilibrium, peace, and interior harmony. Stretching and lengthening muscles that are chronically contracted helps to rebalance both body and mind. What happens in the body affects the mind, just as the mind affects the body. Thus there are two aspects to the practice of yoga postures: the external form or the posture that works through the body, and the internal form that works through the mind. This holistic union of body and mind provides the climate, the "environment," for a spiritual, intuitive experience of God.

The first encounter many Christians have with the East is related to the learning of methods like hatha yoga, tai chi, aikido, zazen—practices that engage the whole person. The practitioners often begin naively and by degrees are drawn in further than they had anticipated because they discover themselves being opened to spirit through this practice. They relate how, for perhaps the first time, they felt "at home" in their bodies, or how they "discovered" their breathing. Their bodily experience draws them into a change of consciousness and leads them toward a deeper experience of conversion.

They usually do not even have words to explain it. But when, through a tea ceremony or sitting in meditation, the mind descends into the heart or the *hara* (abdomen), one looks at the same things in a new way. Something opens within, and there is an experience of renewal. Progress in the spiritual life sometimes comes through a more profound experience of the body. Certain convictions or values that previously were central for us cede their place to other, newly impacting values. Allowing one's faith to take bodily expression in one's whole being is like using a higher octane fuel; the car runs differently in the aftermath. The interplay on this level is more important than we thought. Familiarity with Eastern traditions can stimulate a spiritual practice that encourages Christians to integrate all their faculties more harmoniously "so that God may be glorified in all things" (1 Pet 4:11).[21]

The Christian tradition has analogous though less developed practices such as *hesychasm*, a movement cultivating silence and solitude in Eastern Christianity, or the Spiritual Exercises of Ignatius in Western practice. But overall we have not had the anthropology our theology deserves and requires. In the Hellenistic world in which Christianity evolved, the body was generally regarded as a prison cell in which the soul was trapped. The Greek's relationship to his or her body differed from that of the Semite. But even though the Greek understanding was dominant and pervaded the outlook of the world from which Christianity emerged, Christian notions of incarnation and resurrection constantly challenged it.

The need for such challenge continues. In certain eras of Christian history, the body was ignored; in others, denied. In our era, it is glorified. In different periods of history, Christians have been variously exhorted to mortify their bodies and punish themselves, to control their bodily appetites perceived as hindrances to spiritual development, and to transcend their bodies so as to live in a purely spiritual way. The challenge before us in a secular culture that idolizes the body is not to overcompensate for centuries of misguided teachings—Paul said "Glorify God in your body" (1 Cor 6:20), not "Glorify your body"—but to find a balance between idolatry and denial, between mortification and glorification. Jane Vennard describes what a balanced approach to our embodiment looks like:

> When we are balanced, we treat our bodies as intimate friends. In close friendship, we seek to know the other and at the same time honor the mystery of who the other is. In close friendship, conflict and stress will appear and disappear, giving the relationship a rhythm of its own. Sometimes we will take our friend

for granted, at other times pour great love and energy into the friendship. We know that the friendship changes over time and that we risk stifling its beauty if we hold on too tight. Intimate friendship teaches us about loving and letting go, because we know that the other does not belong to us but has come into our life as a gift. In friendship we make a commitment to that gift. A balanced relationship with our bodies has all these elements of friendship: love, letting go, conflict, change, commitment. We seek to know our bodies while we honor the mystery of our bodies. We attend to our bodies when they are in great need. We also attend when all is going well. We commit ourselves to care for our bodies. We thank God for the body that has been given, for it is the only one we have.[22]

Notes

1. As quoted in Thomas Ryan, *Fasting Rediscovered* (New York/Ramsey, NJ: Paulist Press, 1981), 109–10.

2. Stephanie Paulsell, *Honoring the Body* (New York: Jossey-Bass, 2002), 89.

3. Ronald Rolheiser, *The Holy Longing* (New York: Doubleday, 1999), 79.

4. Ibid., 79–80.

5. World Council of Churches, *Baptism, Eucharist, and Ministry* (Geneva, Switzerland: World Council of Churches, 1982), 12, par. 13.

6. Ibid., par. 19 and 20.

7. George M. Soares-Prabhu, *The Dharma of Jesus* (Maryknoll, NY: Orbis Books, 2003), 196, 197.

8. Ibid., 201.

9. Joseph Blenkensopp, "Theological Synthesis and Hermeneutical Conclusions," in *Immortality and Resurrection*, Pierre Benoit and Roland Murphy, ed., The New Concilium Series (New York: Herder and Herder, 1970), 125.

10. Ibid., 126.

11. John Paul II, *The Theology of the Body According to John Paul II: Human Love in the Divine Plan* (Boston: Pauline Books and Media, 1997).

12. Ibid. See also Christopher West, *The Theology of the Body Explained* (Boston: Pauline Books and Media, 2003).

13. J. Philip Newell, *Echo of the Soul: The Sacredness of the Human Body* (Harrisburg, PA: Morehouse Publishing, 2000), 82.

14. Ibid., 83–84.

15. Ibid., 87–88.

16. Ibid., 89–90.

17. Luke Timothy Johnson, "A Disembodied 'Theology of the Body,'" in *Commonweal* (January 26, 2001), 16.

18. Newell, xvii–xviii.

19. Part One, "The Heart of Buddhist Meditation," in Nyanaponika Thera, *The Heart of Buddhist Meditation* (York Beach, ME: Samuel Weiser, Inc.), 19–113.

20. Andi Young, *The Sacred Art of Bowing* (Woodstock, VT: SkyLight Paths Publishing, 2003), 50–51.

21. Pierre Francois de Béthune, *Faith and Hospitality* (Mahwah, NJ: Paulist Press, 2003), 33–34, 71.

22. Jane E. Vennard, *Praying with Body and Soul* (Minneapolis: Augsburg, 1998), 19–20.

4.

Voices from the Mat

Casey Rock

The outbreak of SARS (Severe Acute Respiratory Syndrome) in Toronto in the spring of 2003 gave both citizens and health professionals cause for concern. It also brought the pattern of human contact into high relief. For the ordinary healthy person who avoided hospitals and flights to the Far East, life pretty much went on as usual. But my own routine was disrupted on two occasions in two different settings, and it prompted some reflection. At the start of the week, the pastor at my local church announced that due to heightened sensitivity about contagion, the kiss of peace should be a nod at one's neighbor and the communion cup would not be passed. A few days later at my yoga class, the teacher declared that for the duration of the outbreak she would not be doing any hands-on assists nor would we be pairing off to help each other, sometimes called "partner" yoga. These "mini-quarantines" led me to wonder if there were any other public places, other than medical facilities, where human beings regularly engaged in benign and peaceable touch. It led me to further ponder my own delicate tango with Christianity and yoga.

Popular culture, if it even acknowledged such a relationship between the two, would say that yoga takes the spotlight for this dance: The churches are emptying; the yoga centers are full, especially on weekends. Yoga is on the front page of magazines and health sections in the newspaper. There are even new forms of yoga being advertised, just in case one is wary of Eastern religions or spiritual connotations. One can find "Hot Power Yoga," "Snowshoeing and Yoga," and "Emotional Yoga." Suffice it to say, yoga has gained wide cultural acceptance; it has even gained respect among those who have never ventured near a class. After I completed my teacher training and had the occasion to tell people I was now a yoga teacher, the general reaction was one of interest and admiration. My graduating class went back home and had little trouble starting classes of their own or working at established yoga centers. But when I completed a master of divinity degree at around the same time, that news, if not a conversation stopper, met with less discernable enthusiasm and more outright confusion. My theological school sent its graduates out into parish environments where attendance continues to dwindle and the likelihood of ministering to people between the ages of twenty and fifty grows slimmer year by year.

But any serious student of yoga soon learns that yoga arose out of a firm belief on the part of its founders that the practice would help them come closer to the divine. Indeed, the primary purpose of yogic physical conditioning on the Indian subcontinent has always been to increase one's ability to pray longer and better. North America has, in many cases, opted to amputate that association. Our predominantly Judeo-Christian culture has been uncomfortable with "whose" divine might be accessed in yoga, and we have a history of understanding God and the body only in negative relationship.

To many people, both in churches and in yoga classes, any comparison between worship and yoga might be odious. Christian churchgoers may feel that what liturgy does and is about is in no way comparable to what a yoga class does and is about. This is somewhat true: liturgy is focused on vocal prayer, on commemoration, on the handing on of tradition, and more recently, on a call to social action. The problem is that such meaning and relevance can only be sustained by what Charles Davis calls "an explicit, personal awareness of the presence of God."[1] Whatever the reason—cultural/societal shifts, education, the growth of democracy, sheer benightedness—Christian churches have lost the authority to arouse or to foster this awareness. Conversely, in the yoga class, students raised in completely secular environments often express a desire for a "spiritual" dimension to their lives. They struggle for a vocabulary to explore or describe their own religious experience. Or some are in "recovery" from a wounding or alienating experience of religious affiliation. For them God-talk is static—it will always bring to mind the negative—while a yoga practice is a respite from polemics. They can still be engaged with the Source of Being without the challenge of faith statements.

I propose that yoga is one place in the culture where the natural, human thirst for contact with God is being satisfied, even if the participants would never use such language. And it is happening there because it is in the body, first and foremost, that God comes. It happens there because the pathway to a primal understanding of one's uniqueness is cleared. Yoga accomplishes this important task, I believe, because it fosters tranquility, cultivates forgiveness, and promotes the feminine.

Yoga and Tranquility

I once taught a yoga class for the staff at a children's science museum. Appropriate space in the building was at a premium and all that was available was a cavernous room where upcoming exhibits were constructed. A few carpenters hammered away in one corner. The walls did not reach the ceiling. We could see and hear children running by on a walkway leading to the mezzanine level. We were visible to them, perhaps as a study in kinetic movement. We could hear and see their excited shouts as they waved to us. We could also hear the squeals of delight from interactive exhibits next door. I strained my voice to be heard during most of the class; a peaceful relaxation time was an impossibility. By mutual agreement, the classes did not resume after an introductory period. I am sure that more benefit was to be had on a Nautilus machine at the local gym, complete with rock music on the headphones, than was to be had on the floor of that museum. I know I needed stress relief by the time the hour was up.

This is not, or should not be, the environment of the best kind of yoga class. In ideal circumstances, the yoga space makes a strong appeal to all the senses, and the major message it delivers is one of calm. Such an ambiance is necessary if one is to quiet the mind and focus on bodily awareness. Attention is paid to space itself. The yoga studio is characterized by a feeling of openness and lack of clutter. In the best of circumstances there is ample room for each body, often lying outstretched, often standing with arms swinging, to move freely. What happens in this space can be very personal; a lifted leg, a thrust-out chest, a deep sigh—all will be seen and heard. To enter into this sort of letting go with any confidence, the individual needs the security of a personal bit of ground and no one breathing down his or her neck.

Most often there is nothing on the walls. In fact, some studios will cover unsightly necessities such as heating ducts or shelving units with swaths of fabric in white or warm colors, in order that the sightlines are neutral and unbroken. Attention is always paid to simplicity and to order. I have noticed with some curiosity how yoga students will freely contribute to the preservation of the peaceful yoga space. They automatically make tidy their personal belongings, stow mats and cushions at the end of class, and would never consider littering. They seem to be guided by a perception of this little oasis as rare and needing cooperation to be preserved.

Yoga teachers are also sensitive to the sources of light in the space. A room full of natural light is ideal, but when artificial light is all that is available, it is used judiciously, mainly for entering and exiting a class. The use of candles and indirect lighting is preferred and commonplace. Students are also frequently instructed to close their eyes during class, primarily at the start and at the end, in order to lasso the wandering mind and to keep the awareness within.

Just as a jangling décor works against the calming of the mind, a cacophony of sound is likewise disturbing. In yoga spaces every attempt is made to temper the noise of vehicular traffic, discordant music, and over-loud voices. Visiting with fellow students before and after class is of course encouraged, but idle chat during the practice is almost always frowned upon. Many yoga teachers make use of background music during the exercises or during the relaxation period. Yoga classes are, after all, one of the places where New Age music got its start! There is a body of study, however, that supports the belief that certain sounds induce or promote receptivity and relaxation. Nature sounds, chants, or electronic rhythms do not engage the intellect. There are no words to stir the emotions and no charismatic performers to offer that kind of distraction.

Yoga teachers themselves are aware of the quality and power of their own voice. They know that a steady, friendly tone supports the atmosphere of trust they are endeavoring to create. In fact, sometimes such a serene attitude and caring demeanor result in the student's placing inappropriate demands on a teacher for attention. Or occasionally students imagine wrongly that the teacher possesses insights that are particularly profound or even supra-human.

In this way yoga disengages us bit by bit from the pressures of the daily grind. The senses are not assaulted. The outside world is allowed in only as fresh air. Perfumes and strongly scented lotions and shampoos are discouraged. The ethos of yoga declares that the human body, as it is made and without adornment, is a wondrous thing. No wonder then that yoga retreats in the Caribbean, Mexico, and Hawaii are so popular. To move with grace and to breathe with awareness in the midst of such lush surroundings is a confirmation of our belonging to the beauty of creation. For yoga, you come as you are. "Fashionable" yoga aside, the yoga practitioner gives little thought to clothing, except to donning what is most comfortable. One wears what will not pinch, not itch, and not reveal too much. Yoga wear, I would argue with Madison Avenue or Rodeo Drive, is anti-fashion. It is as if the mind could ask the human frame what it would like to wear, and the frame answers that it would always choose the favorite, comfy, stay-at-home-and-watch-TV outfit. It answers that because such time is also downtime, the opportunity to let go of personas, to forget obligations. It is that "me" that the teacher hopes shows up for yoga class.

My experience of the oasis of the yoga space tells me that this is one place where the spiritually hungry have fled when there is a disconnect between the longing for inner peace and the older, traditional representations of religious experience. The inner landscape is increasingly difficult to find, and that has to do not only with the pace of modern life but with the rapid disappearance of so much that was familiar. We are continually faced with changing customs, family constructs, work patterns, and the psychic demands of living in a global village. Leonard Cohen says that even the arts cannot respond adequately to our circumstances:

We're in a very shabby moment and neither the literary nor the musical experience has its finger on the pulse of our crisis. We're in the midst of a Flood, and this Flood is of such Biblical proportions that I see everyone holding on in their individual way to an orange crate, to a piece of wood and we're passing each other in this swollen river that has pretty well taken down all the landmarks and overturned everything.[2]

I see the student in the yoga class as someone who has found a way to hold onto one small something in the rushing river of their life. The decision to enter that space is a decision to become quiet and to put on hold any demands other than those they came into the world with — the breath and the movement of the body.

Yoga and Forgiveness

The yoga class does not communicate only by its ambiance. The teacher has a platform and a message to deliver. Reduced to its essentials, it is something very basic, so primitive in fact as to pass unnoticed by most yoga teachers themselves. The message is: "You exist." That may strike our ears very strangely. The yoga student could respond: "Of course, I exist. Who else walked in here and paid for a class?" The teacher is not interested in your checkbook, or your job, or your love life, or where you came from. It is better, in fact, if he or she doesn't know — in order to see more clearly your body: your head, neck, shoulders, waist, hips, legs, feet. How unique, what a relief actually, to be treated simply as a body, to be seen *in* one's body.

What I mean here is something very different from one's body treated as an object. The body is objectified when enslaved, sexually exploited, or pressed into combat. The yoga class celebrates the body as subject. The yoga teacher who sees your body is not like the judge at a beauty contest or a personal trainer at the local gym. That kind of seeing is precipitated by comparison and evaluation. In a pageant, one body will be a "winner"; at the gym, the trainer, at your request, is looking out for where you fall short of the optimum, what areas need to be improved. If there is anything the yoga teacher wishes to change, it is your own perception of yourself. The teacher says, for example, "Become aware of your feet, bend your knees, squeeze your shoulder blades together, lift the crown of your head." All human bodies are built to do this, yours, mine, Madonna's. We have the same raw material—in differing dimensions, granted—but there exists the same potentiality and the same limitations. We cannot walk on our tongues or breathe through our toes. But within this range there is enormous opportunity to wonder at and explore the human body.

Too often when we reach adulthood, we acquiesce to what we think of as a law of diminishing returns. Since the body cannot move exactly as it did in youth, we give up even trying. Or we punish it with over-vigorous aerobic workouts. Perhaps it is true that the current popularity of yoga has to do with a youth-obsessed, anti-aging culture. Maybe it really is just one among other options including wrinkle creams, liposuction, and botox injections. But I doubt that people with such expectations will last very long in yoga practice; visible results of that kind are a long time in coming. What I think is really recovered by adults who turn to yoga is a childlike relationship to their bodies. When, since we were very young, have we been in a room where it is expected that we will play with our toes, see how high we can reach, balance on one foot, maybe even one day try a handstand?

Such a delicate environment can only be established and fostered by a yoga teacher who constantly reinforces the notion that your particular body and what it can do at that moment are perfectly okay. He or she tells you in so many words that every body is unique and you were born with what you were born with. The teacher couples technical knowledge—tall people have tight hamstrings, wide people do not bend easily, men are generally inflexible in the hips, women often have less upper-body strength—with a belief in something the teacher would not name, but I will: forgiveness. The yoga teacher sees the body in front of him or her as it was constructed, but is also conscious of the fact that it has a history. Every body bears scars and wounds, from scrapes and accidents, from the slight to the serious. Some bodies may have undergone invasive surgery. Some may have literally lost parts of themselves. Many have gone through childbirth. Some may presently be living with cancer. Some have had physical violence perpetrated against them. All such experience is still carried in the body. The yoga class is a place where we come up against those memories once again.

There are scars that are physical and others that have their origins solely in the psyche, but those too are carried in the body.

Since the time of Freud, psychoanalysis (and more recently, even general medicine) has been researching the nature of psychosomatic illness. Of late, the terms have changed, and the prevalence acknowledged to be more widespread. For example, now it is readily admitted that people with chronic neck and jaw tension were often prevented from speaking as children. At the very least, most of us would not argue with how excessive stress can make our back and shoulders ache. It is not ludicrous to suggest it can be a result of carrying heavy psychological, not physical, burdens. A yoga teacher, therefore, can be a monitor and a caretaker of our encounter with our past, as well as a gentle guide into our meeting this layered self in the present. A wise yoga teacher negotiates these precarious waters by speaking always of tolerance. Each person is encouraged to move to, but not beyond, his or her limit or capacity. There are no "wrong" moves.

I have made reference to the yoga class as the re-creation of a childlike state, even if only that of our dreams. I would like to extend this analogy as it relates to the idea of forgiveness. In Catholic sacramental theology, before the age of seven a child is not held culpable for his or her actions. Seven was commonly acknowledged to be the age of reason, the stage in human development when one is supposed to be able to distinguish between right and wrong. After this point, if there is any wrongdoing, reconciliation is called for. This process is overseen by the priest, though only God forgives.

I would offer another take on the age of reason, as regards the body. It is around this same time that we all experience a "Fall." We leave our time of happy kindergarten play and go off to full-time school. There the comparisons begin. Some are chosen for sports teams, others not. Girlish activity is defined, and boyish activity too. Our bodies are denounced on the playground. Suddenly appear "the klutz," "the spaz," and "the retard." A host of examiners more exacting than any pageant panel point out the fatties, the faggots, and the losers. Our bodies are suddenly broken off from what we thought (but what was really pre-thought) of as *ourselves*, delightful, whole, smoothly functioning units that were just supremely us. At this time we begin to first really *see* the body, but as if it were an alien and a liar. The body is somehow saying something to others that we have had little reason heretofore (unless at the hand of cruel parents) to have ever sensed or thought about ourselves. Once the closest of partners, my body is no longer reliable as the bearer of "me." And for many years, whether our body is rejected or adored by others, we hide in secret corners the "real" me that no one sees.

It could be that one of the reasons for the popularity of yoga is that in such gatherings people are finding ways, unlike Humpty Dumpty, to put themselves together again. They are provided the space, encouragement, and motivation to meet themselves as they are and to develop attitudes of compassion, patience, and gratitude.

Yoga and Women

At the end of yoga class, it is customary for students to observe with a chuckle that the room has memories of kindergarten. That is because at relaxation time the lights are dimmed and the teacher will offer blankets to those who are feeling a chill—pillows too or eye pads to help more resistant bodies begin to settle down. It reminds many of nap time at preschool. It could be that the laughs cover a certain longing for the simplicity and comfort of those days. Of course, not all childhood memories are soothing. I taught yoga for one summer to the residents of Covenant House, a shelter for runaway and homeless teenagers. The yoga room became a hangout because there you could see candles and incense, popular items with the kids, but both forbidden in their rooms. There, if you obliged the teacher with a little bit of stretching, you could lie down and close your eyes. She played soft sounds of nature and more often than not you drifted off. A runaway shelter is a noisy, tense environment. The potential for some flare-up is always lurking beneath the surface. Young people do not sleep well there. It is not "home," even if their real "home" was not home either, as we like to imagine it. What a yoga space creates, even for a few minutes, is a respite, a momentary sense of being cared for—and that, I believe, is the foundation of a personal awareness of the presence of God.

For most of us the foundational experience of being cared for is that which we received at the hands of our mothers. But not only mothers, women in general, have been the ones who throughout history have seen to the needs of the body and the pleasures of the senses. This is evident in our roles as mothers, wives, lovers, cooks, seamstresses, and midwives. We bathe, brush, massage, cradle, and nurse others. We kiss and make it better. It should come as no surprise then that yoga, as a profession and as a practice, draws a group of people who come to the mind/body/spirit connection instinctively. And while the language here has been inclusive, it should also come as no surprise that, at least in North America, women make up the lion's share of both the yoga-student and yoga-teacher populations. It seems that women have found an arena where they dominate and where a holistic practice can take root, away from the ambitions of the health club and away from the gender dysfunction and bodily unease connected with the major religions.

What has my antennae up are moves to make this nascent outpost of feminine spirituality fit into some pre-existent system. Throughout history the activity of women in this area made those in power nervous. The result was that they stepped in and regulated the activity or they usurped it outright. Presently, the first danger lies with those who are in control of the "beauty" industry. Such investors stand to gain either by making money directly from the growth in yoga, or they stand to gain in an indirect way. The print and visual media and the drug companies, for example, gain when women are neurotically obsessed with body image. Serious practitioners watch in alarm as yoga is pitched as another weapon in the modern woman's assault on perfection. Yoga will help her in the war against flab, wrinkles, and menstrual distress, and the razor-sharp mind that yoga bestows will give her an advantage in boardroom politics.

Secondly, women should be curious about the power of the yoga guru. We ought to be asking ourselves why it is that, while the great majority of practitioners are female, the yoga masters are overwhelmingly male—Iyengar, Desai, Bikram, Yee, and Jois spring to mind. Disregarding what charges of emotional and/or sexual abuse have been levied against some gurus, the question remains why women continue to so often look to men for spiritual insight, distrusting or discounting the value of their own experience.

In the summer of 2001, I was part of a seminar/retreat for yoga teachers interested in exploring the relationship of Christianity to their yoga practice. Nineteen people took part in the event—only six of them were men. Of the conference presenters, one of six was female. Two other women led experiential or reflective evening sessions. To be both clear and fair, the organizer had sent an open invitation to all the participants to speak to the group—it was his intention that it be a self-led, grassroots experience—but primarily it was the men who took him up on it. During our week together, the women mostly led the yoga; the men mostly led the talk. Where were the women's voices? Part of the answer lies in the disconnect between that which is happening in our bodies and that which we believe to be godly. Both Christian women and men suffer from an illiteracy in this regard, but women are additionally inhibited because so few of them have had the kind of theological background that would put them at their ease in a discussion that tries to fit what is happening to them into some sort of religious context.

But the other possibility that deserves consideration is the propensity men have for making a formula out of their experience. The men who presented at the conference tested the validity of what was new and different for them in yoga by laying it out against that which has been purported by other, also predominantly male, thinkers. I am reminded of the image of the old-fashioned transparencies used for demonstration purposes before the age of computers. An acetate sheet with one diagram could be laid over another on an overhead projector, enabling one to observe where figures came together and where they separated. To generalize, in such a way do men accrue insight and in such a way do they communicate it. To continue the generalizing, my observation was that the women came to the conference without a "version" of yoga to project. They came to meet people and to learn and share from each person's story. That story was laid out next to my own story—each was allowed its own richness and was able to stand alone.

The challenge facing women in such circumstances is that we do not have the history, the forum, or the confidence to let "story" be the model for a way of being. Women know the truth of this on some deep level, as they also are aware of the great wisdom that arises from "story." Perhaps it is the fear of such an unwieldy, mysterious power source that contributed to the rise of patriarchy. Perhaps the fact that *one* story by its very definition cannot rule is reason why women have such difficulty in today's power structures. But it is also the reason why we have such a responsibility to work for the eventual dissolution of structures that continue to oppress.

Women are ministering in yoga classes in ways denied to them since the earliest days of Christianity. When Jesus is with women in the New Testament, it is frequently a fleshly encounter. His mother asks him to make sure there is enough wine at a wedding. He asks the woman at the well to quench his thirst. Mary pours costly perfume on his feet and dries them with her hair. Martha confesses to him the stress of an overworked hostess. A woman asks him to stop her pernicious bleeding. Women stand at the foot of the cross and watch him die. Mary Magdalene goes to the tomb to rub his dead body with special oils. How is it that after such mundane, realistic, human encounters with the living Jesus, the Church that is formed after him prohibits women from "sacred" activity? They are not to touch the water, the wine, the bread, or the oils. They may press and mend (but not wear) the sacred garments. There will be no laying on of hands, no therapeutic touch. Female voices used to welcome a child into the world, and female hands embalmed the dead. But in the Church family, the voice that welcomes one in and sends one out is that of a man's. This is so far from real life, from the bodily reality of human exchange for both men and women, that the Church has effectively locked Jesus away. Caroline Bynum tells us what happened in the Middle Ages when women were denied the access that priests had to the Eucharist. They

> encountered in their flesh the body of Christ that was so hard to receive from their male counterparts. In their bodies, through fasting, ascetical practices, stigmata, mystical visions and even mystical unions, women experienced the suffering and redeeming body of Christ. Full integration was found precisely in and through the body.[3]

Conclusion

My local church and the yoga studio where I continue to take classes are six blocks apart on a broad boulevard in downtown Toronto. I often muse on the distance between the two buildings and on what connects them, and how they both relate to the busy "real" world of shops and cafes in between. Despite the negation of the feminine, sometimes I think it was the Church that brought me to yoga. I remember reading James Keenan:

> ...our tradition is extraordinarily physical. While sharing with other traditions belief in God as Creator and in the goodness of the created world, Christianity distinguishes itself by the extraordinary confession of the Incarnation. Likewise, its central liturgy revolves around eating the body and drinking the blood of its Savior, it defines its church as the Body of Christ, and its longstanding hope is in the resurrection of the body.[4]

From a very young age the worship experience stimulated my senses and connected the presence of God to being alive in the body. In that setting I encountered fragrance, song, and candlelight. And while bodies in church moved in small and circumspect ways, they became postures of reverence that expressed humanity's stretch to contact the divine. Even the Christian iconography that surrounded me spoke, yes, of suffering, but also of healing and rejuvenation. I agree with John Bentley Mays' appreciation of Michelangelo, his perception that the cycle from Fall to Judgment in the Sistine Chapel is not an illustration of the bad things sex does to you, "but an illustration that to be in communion with God is to be alive in every sense — morally, intellectually, sexually—while to be cut off from God is to wither."[5] As a young woman I fled from liturgy because of poorly articulated messages from the pulpit on moral theology. The Church and I still struggle with those issues, but now at least I understand that the crisis emerges from the distinct stance Roman Catholicism takes with regard to the connection of God and the human body.

But there are other moments when I think that it is yoga that has saved me. I returned to church in my late thirties to reconnect with my past and to educate my children. I began a practice of yoga around the same time, with the hope of rediscovering my body (at least my navel) after the rigors of childbirth. What I found through yoga was that bodily awareness and breath control did indeed put "me in touch with me" again. I retrieved the wonders and the wisdom that lay within. And while I was regularly brought up against weakness and limitation, at the same time I experienced growth and renewal. Yoga gave me this because of its commitment to quiet space and time, its concepts of acceptance and forgiveness, and the abiding presence of women. The yoga class brought me, brings me, again and again to a primal awareness of my existence and my innate goodness. No words about the divine precede or replace messages such as these.

I described my relationship with Christianity and yoga as a tango. Even though the partners in a tango often dance cheek to cheek, there are moments when they turn their heads away and look stonily in opposite directions. One half of the duo seems not to want to go where he or she is being led. I am reminded of a workshop I attended at the Kripalu Center in Lenox, Massachusetts. I signed up for what was known as a Welcome Weekend, a program designed to give newcomers a taste of Kripalu philosophy, yoga, and hospitality. On arrival I was intrigued to discover that the building and its very beautiful grounds used to be a Jesuit seminary. Under the new ownership the rooms were simply but brightly adorned, and all the public spaces bore no vestige of their former incarnation—except for one. On the second floor was a huge and lovely carpeted space, used for large yoga classes and teachings of the (now departed) guru, but formerly the seminary chapel. However, the current occupants had decided to leave the enormous mosaic representation of St. Ignatius uncovered at the front of the room. It was in that room on the Sunday morning, after a vigorous but excellent yoga session when we were lying in *shivasana*, "corpse" or relaxation pose, that I became aware of tears rolling out the corner of my eyes. I opened them and looked at St. Ignatius, and he too seemed full of sadness and regret. Here was a room filled with people seeking quiet, rejuvenation, connection, centering—possible now that the Christians had left. Kripalu was offering chanting, incense, fasting, and manual labor. They counseled moderation in all things and even abstinence in some things (men and women permanent residents were kept strictly apart in those days), and people could not get enough. On that weekend the residents were scurrying around, decorating the building for the guru's birthday. He would make a rare appearance that night.

Suddenly I wanted very much to be getting ready for my teacher. I wished, childlike, for the serene entrance of a smiling, simply robed Jesus Christ. The weeping Mary Magdalene at the empty tomb sprang to my mind: "They have taken away my Lord, and I do not know where they have laid him" (John 20:13).

For now I must be content with the movement back and forth between church and yoga studio, not minding too much that the gifts of the one have yet to be fully recognized by the other. It was my tradition, after all, that granted me the vocabulary to identify with Mary Magdalene. It was yoga, after all, that made me receptive to hearing those words. For the present, I am grateful to have been invited to the dance.

Notes

1. Charles Davis, *Body as Spirit* (New York: Seabury, 1976), 34.

2. Pico Iyer, "New Life of a Ladies' Man," *The Globe and Mail* (Toronto, ON), May 1, 1999, CO6.

3. From Bynum's *Holy Feast and Holy Fast* (Berkeley, CA: University of California, 1987), paraphrased by James Keenan in "Christian Perspectives on the Human Body," *Theological Studies* 55 (June 1994): 339.

4. Keenan, 345.

5. John B. Mays, "Drying in the Chapel," a review of *Michelangelo and the Pope Ceiling* by Ross King, *The Globe and Mail* (Toronto, ON), March 29, 2003, D28.

5.

The Political and Social Dimensions of Embodied Christian Contemplative Prayer

Jim Dickerson

Enlarge the site of your tent,
    and let the curtains of your habitations be stretched out;
do not hold back; lengthen your cords
    and strengthen your stakes.

(Isa 54:2)

This chapter is about integrating political, social, and earth dimensions into our North American Christian spirituality as the next necessary step in our collective faith-journey. Until we do that, the Church will continue to be unable to respond in its full strength and wisdom to the challenges we face today. We need a spirituality and practice that encompasses the full scope of our richly embodied Christian tradition and biblical theology, one that not only supports us as individuals but also embodies Jesus' alternative social order and prophetic way in a world that operates contrary to it.

For the past thirty-one years I've belonged to an ecumenical Christian church tradition known as Church of the Saviour in Washington, DC. Currently, I am pastor of the New Community Church, which grew out of and stands in the Church of the Saviour tradition. At Church of the Saviour and New Community, we use the terms "inward journey" and "outward journey" to describe our understanding of the Christian life.[1] I came to the Church of the Saviour from Arkansas in 1971 to experience how a local church integrated and structured these two *journeys* into one spiritual practice, in hopes of eventually starting a similar church in Arkansas.

My conscious Christian journey began in 1964 at age twenty-two when, out of a severe personal crisis, I had a profound, life-changing experience of God's healing love. Eventually I came to understand and believe that the full measure of that love was embodied and given in Jesus Christ. While I was not familiar with the terms "inward journey" and "outward journey" at the time of my conversion, I intuitively knew that the change I was experiencing involved both an inward (personal) and outward (social) dimension and that they were two inseparable parts of one experience.

It was not easy back then to find other Christians who shared this understanding, or spoke of the Christian life in these terms. The churches I attended focused their programs, preaching, teaching, and praying around one or the other journey but never both woven together in a coherent balanced program for spiritual growth and ministry. Most churches emphasized the inward journey (personal faith, piety, and salvation) to the exclusion of the outward journey, while a few others emphasized the outward journey (mission, social change, and action) and minimized the inward journey. The groups either didn't know how to integrate the two, felt it was too overwhelming a task, or didn't believe in the importance and need for it. The inward/outward dimensions of the Christian gospel and life were always spoken of and treated as very distinct and separate components.

Mixing Politics and Personal Faith

Fortunately for me there was one significant exception—the Civil Rights Movement led by the African American church in the South and Dr. Martin Luther King, Jr. I've always considered myself fortunate to have been "born again" in the early 1960s, when this country was caught up in the throws of a tumultuous social revolution and spiritual rebirth. While I was undergoing the initial phases of a powerful and thorough personal transformation, the unjust society I was born and raised in was also undergoing a death and resurrection of its own. The Civil Rights Movement gave me a model and structure for expressing both the inward and outward dimensions of my new spirituality in Christian community. God was simultaneously changing everything—personal and social—and there was no separation of the two. Social action and one's personal relationship with God were considered parts of one act of faith, worship, and prayer.

THE POLITICAL AND SOCIAL DIMENSIONS

One dimension was a natural and essential expression of the other, and vice versa.

But taking unpopular public stands against issues like racism, poverty, and war was costly. Churches lost members. Some of my Presbyterian minister friends regularly received death threats and pictures of "gun sights" sent to them in the mail by the Ku Klux Klan because of their efforts to dismantle racial segregation in Little Rock.

In 1964 I quit my secure job at the telephone company and went to work for a local Boys Club in North Little Rock, Arkansas. The Boys Club was in the initial stages of racially integrating its membership. As a result, many of the white kids stopped coming, funding began to dry up, and the director, a committed Christian, came under criticism.

As I began my faith journey, I learned that unless our personal faith and prayer practice moves us beyond charity toward a deep, compassionate, costly engagement with the world and struggle for social change and justice, something fundamental is missing from it. We are dealing with only a portion of the gospel. Our spirituality is not whole. There is a big difference between charity and justice. Charity is about responding to the emergencies, crises, and basic human needs of those we often categorize as the less fortunate. To be sure, charity is important and necessary. Justice, on the other hand, is about changing the social structures and systems that create and perpetuate endemic social problems such as homelessness, poverty, hunger, disease, crime, and violence.

Today, many people are searching for more than what this rational, mechanistic, and materialistic secular world of ours has to offer. We are living in an age when notions of spirituality and following a spiritual path are very popular. There are many different spiritualities, teachers, leaders, and healers, all offering their particular remedies for what ails and alienates us. Our culture's current spiritual climate could be compared to first-century Athens, when Paul toured that city and found a vast array of statues, icons, and temples representing the plethora of gods worshipped and spiritualities practiced there. He even found one icon named for the "unknown god," just in case there was a god they hadn't heard of yet (Acts 17:16–34).

In keeping with this trend over the past twenty to thirty years, the Christian church in this country has rediscovered many of its own historical spiritual traditions and practices and has been busy packaging and promoting them for popular consumption. For example, the "Centering Prayer" movement in this country is a recovery of an ancient prayer tradition developed by third-century Middle Eastern and North African Christians known as "the desert fathers and mothers."[2]

While these traditions and practices are helpful in assisting one to energize and enrich one's personal prayer life, I've observed that, unfortunately, most present-day spiritual programs, Christian and non-Christian alike, speak primarily to the personal and psychological dimensions of the spiritual journey. By and large, they continue to be highly individualistic to the exclusion of the social and political dimensions of the faith journey. I don't know of many contemporary programs, schools of thought, or teachers of spiritual formation and growth who seriously attempt to integrate and give equal emphasis to the political and social dimensions of their particular approaches. If per chance the outward and social dimension is mentioned, it's usually as an awkward afterthought, an obligatory add-on, or is treated separately, but never as an integral and balanced part of the whole presentation, program, and practice.

The Lack of Integration Between Personal Spiritual Practice and Social Justice

My Yoga Teacher-Training at Kripalu

A few years ago, I took a yoga teacher-training course at the Kripalu Yoga Center in Lenox, Massachusetts. The training was rigorous and was excellent preparation for teaching Kripalu's particular approach. During the training, I observed that there was no mention of how Kripalu's brand of yoga and spirituality related to social change and the struggle for justice beyond individual deeds of charity and service to the poor. Most of the participants in my class at Kripalu were good, caring folk, generally middle- to upper-class and politically moderate to liberal. Many were engaged in the helping professions or socially worthwhile endeavors either on a volunteer or professional basis. I didn't meet anyone who was opposed to helping the poor or people in need. But the whole Kripalu program was oriented around individual spirituality, psychosomatic growth, and improvement on an individual basis only. The Kripalu program and curriculum paid little or no attention to how personal change, through its style of yoga and spirituality, is related to social change and justice. When I raised

121

this question with the leaders and teachers, I was told they believed their focus on personal change would somehow eventually have the effect of changing the society. But it was left up to the individual to figure it out and apply as each one saw fit. There was no clear strategy, articulation, or emphasis linking the two together as essential parts of one practice.

My Stress Reduction Training at University of Massachusetts Hospital

A few years ago, I attended a popular stress-reduction program at the University of Massachusetts Hospital in Worcester, Massachusetts. The program was founded and directed by Dr. Jon Kabat Zinn, whose helpful work on the interrelationship between emotional stress and certain physical diseases had been prominently featured in one of Bill Moyer's PBS specials on the topic. The Worcester program taught the participants a Zen Buddhist form of meditation and philosophy and introduced them to a few basic yoga postures over a six- to eight-week period.

I was especially interested in the U. Mass program because one of the classes was located in a lower-income neighborhood and intentionally reached out to poor people. I was hopeful that I could learn something that would assist me in bringing similar resources to lower-income communities in Washington, DC. To my disappointment, the program was focused exclusively around the individual to the exclusion of the social context and environmental conditions in which the lower-income participants lived. A high percentage of the participants repeated the program multiple times, and there was little recognition from most of the staff and leadership of the need to enlarge their "holistic" focus and include the social and environmental causes of stress and disease as well. In discussions with staff and leadership about this issue, I was told in no uncertain terms that their program was focused solely on the individual and not the social conditions in which the individuals lived. They felt that they were teaching individuals how to better cope with their social conditions as they were, regardless of whether those conditions ever changed.

Centering Prayer

For the past twenty years, I have been a practitioner of what's commonly known in this country as Centering Prayer. I am extremely grateful for it and have derived many personal benefits from this way of praying. But I have found its scope and orientation—as currently formulated, taught, and practiced—to be narrowly focused around the personal and psychological, to the exclusion of the human body and the broader social aspects of Christian prayer and contemplation. Teachers of Centering Prayer in the United States, such as Father Thomas Keating, use a "true self/false self" paradigm to describe the inner psychological dynamics at work in the individual as he or she prays and meditates. As I understand it, the goal of this type of prayer is personal and psychological transformation. Over time, Centering Prayer seeks to move the practitioner from being overly attached to and living out of what's termed the false or impermanent self—with its programs for happiness, acceptance, and affection that are based in the emotional traumas of childhood experiences and our being loved conditionally—toward the true or permanent self with its center and source for happiness in God's love disclosed and given in Jesus. Centering Prayer teaches that the false self and its programs for happiness are a product of many forces in society and culture by which we have been negatively influenced throughout our lives. As helpful as this approach is on an individualistic level, it does not take the next step and apply its paradigm for individual transformation to the social and political realms of life in which the individual is related, formed, and shaped.

Prayer of Heart and Body

Similarly, for the past eight years I have been a practitioner and teacher of "The Prayer of Heart and Body," pioneered by Father Tom Ryan, Director of the Paulist North American Office for Ecumenical and Interfaith Relations in New York City. Prayer of Heart and Body (PHB) expands the Christian meditative prayer practice and makes it much more holistic by including the human body through yoga as an integral part of an individual's way of praying. PHB is an "embodied" way of praying that emphasizes the integration of body, mind, and spirit in prayer and Christian living. I have derived enormous benefits from this approach as well as the support and friendship I've found with others who also practice and teach it. One of the greatest benefits has been my growing awareness of my connection to earth and the intimate presence of God reflected and communicated through the physical, material universe. Our human bodies and the earth's body are deeply connected through God, who is embodied in both. As my good friend Dr. Jim Hall says, "Body is earth!" and as the psalmist says, "The earth is the Lord's and all that is in it, the world and all those who live in it" (Ps 24:1). PHB has given me a way to pray with my whole body and not just from my shoulders up. It also has increased my awareness of the divine in relation to social structures, orders, and systems of life. Up until this point in time, however, PHB has been primarily conceptualized and practiced on a very individualistic basis. It has not expanded to include the broader social, political, ecological, and cosmic dimensions of embodiment prayer in a cohesive, balanced, well-integrated manner.

Institutionalized Christianity

In the same way, much of the spirituality that North American Christianity currently promotes continues to ignore the social and political dimension of the gospel and does not effectively integrate systems-change and social-justice aspects into its programs of spiritual formation and growth. The Christian Church is confronted with two problems: (1) the lack of willingness to confront the self-serving, often violent and coercive social systems of society; and (2) the organizational fragmentation and compartmentalization that separates prayer and personal spirituality from social justice and action.

The Church as a whole seems to have little or no interest in fundamentally changing or challenging a system and social order from which the institution and its members derive a great deal of comfort, privilege, and security. Much of the mainline Church seems blind to the ways in which social systems and public policies contradict the gospel of Christ. It's as though we Christians are caught in systems that keep us unconscious and blind to our complicity. It seems easier, safer, and simpler to keep the focus on individual spiritual formation, change, and growth than to include the political and social dimensions of the gospel as integral to our spiritual practice and Christian faith. To expand and integrate the social and political components pushes us out of our comfort zones and challenges us at the point of our privilege, power, security, values, and lifestyles.

In most local churches and parishes, the inward and outward journeys are divided into two or more committees, such as the "social concerns" committee and the "spiritual life" or "Christian education" committee. Prayer groups meet at one time, social action groups meet at another, and they are comprised of different people. While the committees are under the umbrella of one church organization, they are almost always seen as very separate activities and seldom, if ever, are brought together as one function by the same group of people. Social action is usually seen as social services and works of charity. Social justice and systems change is hardly ever seen as an integral part of the committees.

Indeed, mainstream, institutionalized Christianity is currently living in and through an age of accommodation and complicity with the culture and government, or "exile," as Walter Brueggemann puts it, and the spirituality it promotes and practices is a reflection of this compromised state of affairs.[3] We've gotten used to living in our own modern day "Babylon" and assimilated ourselves into an American culture whose values, lifestyles, practices, and patterns are foreign to authentic biblical spirituality and life in Christ. Many expressions of church have Christianized America's ethic of "rugged individualism" and adopted it as its official spirituality. But this compartmentalized, highly individualistic, enculturated spirituality is foreign to the Bible and to the spirituality Jesus is recorded to have practiced. It is very detrimental and disempowering for the Church and those who practice it.

Expanding the Practice

My hope and call is that, just as we have expanded the Centering Prayer practice through PHB to include the human body, we will now take the next natural step toward an even more embodied and holistic prayer practice by integrating the political, social, and earth dimensions. Until that happens, our North American Christian spirituality will continue to be too small, fragmented, and not nearly substantial enough to meet the challenges we face today. We need a spirituality and practice that encompasses the full scope of our richly embodied Christian tradition and biblical theology, one that is holistic and strong enough not only to hold us up and help us cope as individuals in these difficult times, but also, by faith, to embody Jesus' alternative social order and prophetic way in a world that operates contrary to it. We need a spirituality that is, as Paul says, stronger and more powerful than what the world considers strong and powerful (1 Cor 2:18–31). What has gone before is not adequate for what is needed now and in the future. We need an expanded formulation of divine embodiment that integrates and expresses the social, ecological, and cosmic as well as the individual nature of our mystically embodied union and communion with God in Christ. To do this, PHB will need to expand beyond its individualistic focus on yoga and meditation and include the political, social, and natural world dimensions of our embodied tradition. Prayer of Heart and Body will need to become a more comprehensive prayer of embodiment.

Efforts to Integrate and Expand at New Community Church and Manna, Inc.

It's one thing to criticize and point out problems, but always another to do something constructive about them and institute the changes one is calling for in one's life and organizations. Jesus is pretty hard on those who demand of others what they are unwilling to do themselves (Matt 23:3–4). I offer the following account as an example of the imperfect attempt of our congregation to do what we are calling others to do, that is, integrate into our personal lives, work, relationships, and faith communities a healthy balance between personal faith, prayer, and social justice.

In our New Community Church of the Saviour tradition, the inward and outward journeys are woven into our core membership commitments as seamless parts of an overall structure and approach to membership. We have specific spiritual disciplines that involve practicing and integrating both dimensions in the context of small groups, called "mission groups." All mission group members make commitments to a common set of inward and outward spiritual disciplines, for which we hold each other accountable. Each week mission group members submit a written "spiritual report" to another member who serves as the group's spiritual director. Among other things, the report includes a brief accounting of whether we were faithful in keeping our commitments. The report is not a spiritual score card in which we receive a performance grade. Rather, it's a tool for reflection, support, accountability, and feedback from the director to help us realize our desires for growth and a deeper, more consistent spiritual practice in Christian community. I can safely say that hardly anyone ever reports 100 percent success in keeping his or her commitments and maintaining a perfect balance between the inward and outward journeys. We emphasize not "success" or "failure," but faithfulness to the practice.

The Prayer of Heart and Body Mission Group

After participation in my first PHB retreat with Tom Ryan in 1996, I knew I wanted to incorporate PHB in my personal life and offer it as a resource in our church and community. Eventually, I formed a PHB mission group for those in the church and neighborhood who shared a similar interest and calling. Our PHB mission group has been meeting for the past four years each Tuesday morning. Our meetings consist of thirty minutes of yoga and stretching, followed by twenty minutes of meditation. The meeting concludes with discussion of a scripture reading and personal sharing and prayers. Currently, six members are committed to the daily PHB disciplines and outreach ministry of the group, as well as provide mutual support and accountability to one another for the daily practice. Our outreach consists of organizing an annual five-day PHB retreat, conducting periodic classes, drop-in sessions, and special events, and finding ways to incorporate the practice into various areas of our lives, work, and relationships.

Recently, our group worked on trying to be more specific and intentional about integrating the political and social-justice dimensions into the practice and discipline. As a result, we decided to require each member to name and actively participate in some social/systemic change effort as an equally valued and clearly stated aspect of our spiritual disciplines. It was left up to each individual to choose which effort to be involved in and to what degree. As we talked, it quickly became obvious that each member was already involved in some (several!) such ventures.

To our delight, this did not require an additional time commitment for any of us, just more intention and conscious integration of it into our thinking, speaking, acting, and way of praying. We realized that this integration is not as large and overwhelming a task as we thought it might be. For most, it is a simple matter of turning our conscious intention toward the social and political dimensions of the gospel, integrating these dimensions into our personal practice, and structuring them into our faith communities along with other disciplines. When we begin to speak and think of the social and political as equally important as the personal dimension, we experience an enhanced richness, unity, and power in our spirituality.

Manna, Inc.

Along with pastoring New Community Church, I also help direct and manage a nonprofit, affordable-housing and community-development program in Washington, DC, called Manna, Inc. Over the past twenty-one years, we have produced approximately eight hundred homes for ownership by lower-income, first-time homebuyers. When we completed our one hundredth home several years ago, we commissioned a study to see how our buyers liked their new homes and the difference it had made in their lives. Essentially all of the buyers said that "they loved their homes, but hated their neighborhoods." That study helped Manna expand its focus and efforts to include improving the entire neighborhood as well as working with individual families in order to ensure their success.

To date, we have had a total of five foreclosures out of approximately eight hundred homes sold to lower-income folks, far below the national average. This success can be attributed in part to our emphasis on the importance of addressing the problems of the surrounding social environment in which our individual homebuyers live, as well as counseling and training them to be successful on an individual basis. We now do community organizing to help residents discover and use their power in changing social conditions like crime, violence, poor city services, low-achieving schools, addiction, inadequate health care, abandoned and derelict housing, lack of retail business, and displacement due to gentrification, unemployment, and unaffordable housing. Through Manna's Community Development Corporation, we also develop small neighborhood businesses that create jobs and training for residents. Manna has come to realize the importance of focusing efforts on the larger social and political issues, as well as assisting people on an individual basis. Both are essential and interrelated components for transformation.

Dominic Moulden is a member of the PHB mission group and the director of Manna Community Development Corporation. He is a longtime DC resident and justice activist who is leading Manna's efforts to maintain and build racial, economic, and cultural diversity in a rapidly gentrifying, historic, African American neighborhood called Shaw. Dominic leads his staff to organize lower-income people and help ensure that they have a strong political voice for addressing larger social-justice issues affecting their lives. Advocating for economic justice, they work to influence government to enact public policies and provide resources so that the positive changes now occurring in the neighborhood benefit poor people, rather than displace them due to escalating prices. Dominic is also an advocate for institutional change, justice, and compassion in the Roman Catholic Church, of which he is an active member.

Another member of the PHB mission group, Jackie Hart, is also a longtime neighborhood resident and justice advocate. Jackie owns and manages her own small business, House of Hart, a manufacturer of sewn textile products. She is also founder of

SiNGA, a nonprofit organization that provides fashion and textile design training for those interested in becoming employed or entrepreneurs in this field. Jackie serves on the Manna Board of Directors and is involved in advocating for more resources for affordable housing, equitable neighborhood development, and employment and training opportunities for lower-income, underserved residents.

The Theology of Divine Embodiment in Christian Spiritual Practices

In his book *God and Creation*, Jürgen Moltmann quotes Friedrich Oetinger's thesis, "The end of all God's work is embodiment."[4] That is, both God's home and our experience of God are embodied in the entire physical, material universe, including nature and the structures of society, as well as in the enfleshed spirits we call human beings. The principle of divine embodiment, or what is more commonly referred to in Christian theology as "the incarnation," is deeply rooted in the scriptures, as Tom Ryan explains in his book *Prayer of Heart and Body*:

> The central thrust of the Gospel is the proclamation of fullness of life, fullness of being: "I came that you might have life and have it abundantly" (Jn. 10:10). The New Testament witnesses to the transforming impact when people live their lives out in the power of God's love.

"The Kingdom of God is among you" (Lk. 17:21), Jesus announced. This kingdom [this fullness of life and being] is not so much a place as an experience, and eternal life has to do not so much with the duration of time as with depth, richness, intensity and fullness of living....

It is to this awareness that true contemplation leads: we cannot separate God from God's creation.[5]

Further, in *Wellness, Spirituality and Sports*, Tom emphasizes the importance and impact of the incarnation—

The unbelievableness [of the incarnation] perhaps is what influenced John the evangelist in his Gospel prologue to choose the unique phrasing that the Word of God became, not a human being, not even a human person, but *flesh*....

In the face of our devaluations of the flesh that embodies God and the earth which is God's home, God sent us a message: henceforth, God *is identified with and discovered within this bodiliness, this fleshiness, this materiality, [this earthiness], this sensuality, this worldliness, this passion.*[6]

God's earthy, fleshly embodiment radically challenges the Church's destructive practice of compartmentalizing and separating the spiritual life from the physical life. People are generally surprised to hear that Christianity, of all the great world religions, has one of the highest theologies and valuations of the human body and of life in community with others and the earth. Christianity and its spirituality can best and uniquely be described as essentially embodied or incarnational by nature. We believe in the "resurrection of the body" (1 Cor 15), the "body of Christ" (1 Cor 10:16), the "glorification of God in our bodies" (1 Cor 20), the "incarnation" (John 1:14), the "good creation" (Gen 1:4–31), the "new heavens and new earth" (Rev 21:1), and the body as the "temple of the Holy Spirit" (1 Cor 6:19). Yet, sadly, Christianity has neither known nor practiced its own teaching in this regard throughout history, with disastrous consequences in all realms of life.

In reclaiming this rich biblical Christian tradition of divine embodiment, I want to emphasize that I am not saying our God is solely identified with earth and material universe, nor is it my intention to make a god of creation. Our biblical tradition teaches that God is the Creator, separate and not dependent on creation as creation is upon God. But creation, as well as this earthly, historical life, is the primary mode through which our triune God has chosen to disclose and relate to us. Unfortunately, for a variety of reasons, notions of divine separateness (transcendence) and relatedness (immanence or intimacy) in Christian faith and practice have become unbalanced. In some circles, the scales have been tipped on the side of divine separateness, while others have emphasized relatedness and intimacy.

Embodied Christian contemplative prayer seeks to restore a healthy balance between the two and take us deeper into the reality of both. The prayer of embodiment helps recover this balance by involving the human body, the psyche, the earth, and the social structures and orders of life as integral, equally valued components and expressions of our prayer life and experience of God. It opens us up to a more inclusive and holistic spiritual practice—a "spirituality of embodiment." This is good news— healing and hope for those who have been alienated from their own bodily temples of the Holy Spirit and the Creator's presence through the creation. It is also good news for those who have struggled to find a spiritual practice that integrates the social and political dimensions of the gospel into their personal faith and prayer practice.

Practicing Prayer of Embodiment

In personal times of praying with my heart and body, I imagine the practice as a weight I tie around my waist and the time spent stretching and meditating as my taking a big "leap of faith" into the vast mystical ocean of God's unconditional, non-violent, and nondominating love disclosed in Jesus. The practice is a "weight" that I trust takes me down into the mysterious, silent depths of God's loving presence connecting me to all of creation and a deeper rhythm—God's rhythm in Christ pulsating in the depths of life and my inner being. Individual times of embodied contemplative prayer awaken and refine our sensitivities to this deeper current, rhythm, and connection of which we are not normally all that aware. John Dunne powerfully and poetically describes this deeper rhythm and current to which our prayer practice takes us, in his study *Time and Myth*.

An enduring life, a life that could last through and beyond death would have to be a deeper life than the ordinary. It would have to be some life that men [and women] have without knowing it, some current that runs far beneath the surface. To find it would be like seeing something fiery in the depths of life; it would be like hearing a rhythm in life that is not ordinarily heard. The question is whether a [person], if he found such a life, could bear to live it, whether he could live at that depth, whether he could live according to that rhythm. The deeper life would be like an undertow, like a current that flows beneath the surface, a current that sets seaward or along the beach while the waves on the surface are breaking upon the shore....There is no swelling and breaking in the undertow, no foam, no splash, no sound. Yet it is a powerful current and may move in a direction opposite to that of the waves, may move toward the open sea while they move toward the shore. A [person] who gave himself to the deeper current of life might run a risk like that of a man who let himself be caught in the undertow. It might be better for [that person] to float on the surface and let himself be carried in to shore. To live in accord with the deeper rhythm might be to ignore the surface rhythm of life. It might mean missing the normal joys and cares of childhood, youth, [adult]hood, and age. It might mean plunging down into the depths of life to follow a light as elusive as sea fire.[7]

Embodied, contemplative Christian prayer connects us with a power and direction that runs counter to the culture and the way power is normally constituted in us and the society. Our intention in this form of prayer is to freely choose to let go of power as understood by the world's dominant consciousness and domination systems. Our prayer practice takes us to an inner place of being and nondoing—a place that the world would call "powerless." We Christians call that place "justification by faith through grace alone" (Rom 3:21–28).

Taking up residence in this inner place calls into question and undermines many of the foundational principles upon which the world and our culture normally operate and depend on to maintain power, control, and influence in our lives and life in general. Karl Barth said, "To fold the hands in prayer is the beginning of an uprising against the disorder of the world."[8] It's in the *doing* and *possessing* and *fear of letting go* that our culture and its systems thrive and depend, rather than in the *trusting, letting be,* and *letting go* that our prayer practice and Sabbath tradition teach. The prayerful act of consciously letting go and literally withdrawing from the normal patterns, rhythms, routines, values, behaviors, systems, and structures of this life on retreats, in daily prayer times, or on a weekly Sabbath day has radical political and social implications associated with it that we seldom recognize or are willing to acknowledge. Over time and in faithfulness to the practice, the lines between set times of prayer and our public activities slowly begin to merge into two aspects of one seamlessly embodied, countercultural prayer practice and act of faith.

THE POLITICAL AND SOCIAL DIMENSIONS

During Lent of 2003 several of us at New Community Church felt called to gather each Wednesday morning at 7:00 a.m. for a short session of PHB and then adjourn to a location near the U.S. Capitol where we passed out leaflets inviting prayers for peace and advocating alternatives to military violence and war in Iraq. This activity felt as though our public advocacy and demonstration was but an extension of our private PHB practice. They were two integral parts of one embodied prayer practice.

For me, participants in these Wednesday-morning vigils model a healthy integration of personal faith and social action. Retired from full-time work in outreach to isolated, low-income, elderly residents in our neighborhood, Marilyn McDonald is a member of the PHB mission group. Since the tragedy of 9/11, she has intensified her concern for world peace by engaging in a more thorough study of scriptures concerning the nature and uniqueness of God's peace in Christ; she also has intensified her prayers for peace. She has shared the fruit of this inward journey with New Community Church and other congregations, as well as publically witnessing to it during our regular Wednesday-morning vigils and other antiwar demonstrations.

Another member of our Wednesday-morning prayer vigil group is Johan Hammerstrom. Johan is a committed practitioner of PHB but not a member of the PHB mission group. He is employed as a supervisor in an innovative, for-profit information technology services company called Community IT Innovators (CITI). CITI provides affordable computer support services for many of the small nonprofit organizations in

Washington, DC. Johan has organized fellow workers at CITI to show up at affordable-housing lobby days at the DC City Council and Mayor's office. His letters to the editor advocating affordable housing, economic justice, and preservation of diversity in gentrifying neighborhoods have been published in local newpapers. He writes e-mails, makes phone calls to politicians, encourages others to become justice and peace advocates, and joins in public demonstrations for alternatives to war and violence. He is also an advocate for making private-sector, for-profit businesses more public-service oriented and responsive to the needs of the community.

The Rev. Gordon Cosby, cofounder and pastor of Church of the Saviour, once said, "To personally and by faith belong to Jesus Christ and be a member of His Body is the most profound political act one can make." For the Christian, the essence and effect of our embodied contemplative prayer discipline is that of deepening our *inward and outward* lives in Jesus. The divine/human alternative Jesus embodied in his life, death, and resurrection, and made available to us through the Holy Spirit, is the alternative consciousness and countercultural social order into which our embodied prayer practice leads us. Indeed, for the Christian, *Jesus* is the deeper rhythm that runs counter to the surface rhythm in life. It is *Jesus'* alternative rhythm we get caught up in as we deepen our lives in him through this holistic way of praying.

Praying as Jesus Prayed

The Politics of Jesus' Spirituality

In the first chapter of the Gospel of Mark, Jesus' public ministry begins to take off. He's experiencing much initial success and popularity. He's healing and teaching with power and authority and beginning to attract big crowds. Many people are coming to hear his message and be healed of whatever ails them. He is becoming extremely popular and busy. Then in the midst of all this activity, we read these words,

> In the morning, while it was still very dark, [Jesus] got up and went out to a deserted place, and there he prayed. And Simon and his companions hunted for him. When they found him, they said to him, "Everyone is searching for you." He answered, "Let us go on to the neighboring towns so that I may proclaim the message there also; for that is what I came out to do." And he went throughout Galilee, proclaiming the message in their synagogues and casting out demons. (Mark 1:37–39)

In reflecting on this passage, Henri Nouwen once said that the more he read this nearly silent sentence in Mark locked in between the loud words of action and doing, the more he had the sense that the secret of Jesus' life and vocation was hidden in that lonely, deserted place where he very often went to pray early in the morning long before dawn. In the lonely, deserted place

Jesus found courage to hear God's will for his life and not his own; courage to speak God's words and not his own; courage to follow God's will and not his own; and courage to do God's work and not his own.[9]

I would add that surely Jesus also found courage and strength *not* to conform to what others—such as his family, friends, religious and political leaders, and the system he grew up in—wanted him to say and do when it conflicted with his understanding of God's call and direction.

In that lonely and deserted place of prayer where he often went in the early morning hours, Jesus detached from a world—a system, society, culture, and religion—that is organized around distinctions and differences, differences concerning who you are, what you have, where you come from, your status, vocation, and position in life and society, including exclusive and discriminatory categories based upon birth, race, gender, age, religion, nationality, class, mental and physical condition, and profession. This system operated to the political and economic benefit of an elite, wealthy few and to the detriment and expense of the many destitute and poor. This sounds eerily similar to the global society we live in today. According to one study, the richest 20 percent of global society own 89 percent of the world's wealth.[10] Of the remaining 80 percent, more than half (3 billion people) live on less than $2 per day. In the United States today, the wealthiest 5 percent of the population own 59.4 percent of the wealth.[11]

In the lonely place of solitude and prayer, these disparities, these distinctions, and this system are turned upside down and placed in reverse order. In prayer, Jesus disconnects from the system and way of operating controlled by and benefiting a few, while the many are excluded. He disconnects from a world where human worth and value are based primarily on doing rather than being (Luke 10:38–42), on works rather than grace (Luke 18:9–14), on charity rather than justice (Mark 10:17–31), and on holiness rather than compassion (Luke 6:36, 10:25–37).

These alternative principles include unconditional, nonviolent love and unlimited forgiveness for friend and foe alike (Matt 5:38–48; 18:21–22); prophetic compassion (Matt 9:36; 14:14); and a just and inclusive society with an inverted social pyramid and order where the last and least are the first and most important ones of all (Matt 19:30). It's the Kingdom of God *on earth* as it is in heaven! It's Shalom *on earth* as it is in heaven!

Mary Lee Barker and Dorothy Copps are also members of our PHB mission group and embody these alternative principles, rhythm, and system in their lives and work. Mary Lee is an artist and musician who uses her gifts in the cause of peace, justice, community building, and resolving conflict through nonviolent means. In 1988, Mary Lee returned from one of many trips to El Salvador where she both learned from and shared her gifts with people struggling for peace and justice in that country.

Upon her return home, she quietly began painting watercolor portraits of men, women, and children who attended a local soup kitchen known as Loaves and Fishes. As friendships and trust grew between Mary Lee and the folks who attended the program, more and more people wanted Mary Lee to paint their portrait and to listen to their wisdom, experience, and life stories. The portraits are magnificent, and unique in that they often capture the person's story—their inner and outer dignity and beauty—as well as the pain of the person's life. Mary Lee also has encouraged people at the soup kitchen to join with her in advocating for systemic change and justice for themselves and their needs by helping them register to vote and attend marches and rallies for peace and justice.

Dorothy is an assistant to mentally challenged people in L'Arche, and has the role of Home Life Coordinator in one of two group residences. She advocates for person-centered planning for people with disabilities in the L'Arche community, as well as in other city-run day programs and at one of the primary organizations that fund programs such as L'Arche. Dorothy and her husband, Tom, are very active in their inner-city neighborhood, building community across lines of separation such as race and class. They are active in organizing neighborhood efforts to reduce crime, violence, and devastation due to illegal drug activity and addiction.

Praying as Jesus Prayed:
A Forty-Day Retreat in the Desert

Then Jesus was led up by the Spirit into the wilderness to be tempted by the devil. He fasted forty days and forty nights, and afterwards he was famished. The tempter came and said to him, "If you are the Son of God, command these stones to become loaves of bread." But he answered, "It is written,

'One does not live by bread alone,

but by every word that comes from the mouth of God.'"

Then the devil took him to the holy city and placed him on the pinnacle of the temple, saying to him, "If you are the son of God, throw yourself down for it is written,

> 'He will command his angels concerning you,'
>> and 'On their hands they will bear you up,
> so that you will not dash your foot against a
>> stone.'"

Jesus said to him, "Again it is written, 'Do not put the Lord your God to the test.'"

Again, the devil took him to a very high mountain and showed him all the kingdoms of the world and their splendor; and he said to him, "All these I will give you, if you will fall down and worship me." Jesus said to him, "Away with you, Satan! For it is written,

> 'Worship the Lord your God,
>> and serve only him.'"

Then the devil left him, and suddenly angels came and waited on him.

(Matt 4:1–11)

This story gives us a very clear picture of the two rhythms and currents in life previously mentioned. Moving in one direction are the surface rhythm and current represented by Satan's offerings to Jesus. Moving in the opposite direction are the deeper current and rhythm represented by Jesus' responses. Usually Jesus' temptations in the desert are interpreted in a very personal and psychological manner, but these passages are also profoundly political and social. Satan makes Jesus an offer that no one in his right conventional mind can refuse: "an entire nation's [Israel's] collective, popular messianic hopes and aspirations."[12] In essence, Satan says, "Worship me and I will enable you to feed all the hungry people in the world, give you a chance to vindicate Yahweh's honor by jumping off the tower of the temple and landing unhurt, and give you power over all the kingdoms of the world." In Jesus' time, Israel's God had been derided and discredited as weak in comparison to other nations' gods because Yahweh appeared not to be able to deliver Israel from Roman domination. Israel's messianic hopes and expectations were clearly and compellingly spelled out to Jesus by Satan on this forty-day retreat.

Jesus knew the deep national longings of his people. He knew the scriptures, the beliefs, tradition, hopes, and expectations of his community. The temptations he struggled with were real, potent, and lethal. What Jesus was offered were the essential tools for achieving and maintaining power in the world. We know the struggle! The temptations are the "surface rhythm," "the foam," "the splash" of this world's systems and consciousness rolling onto the shore of Jesus' consciousness and messianic vocation, beckoning him to go in that direction. Jesus was presumably well aware that God's will, as popularly understood, meant Israel's freedom from the hated Roman occupation and domination; restoration of God's nation (Israel) as in the time of David; and vindication of Yahweh's honor. The Messiah was to be a spiritually endowed, politically shrewd military man who would reverse Israel's misfortunes through military might. Sounds surprisingly familiar and agonizingly close to home, doesn't it![13] Jesus chooses instead to say "yes" to God's alternative consciousness and nonviolent domination-free system. In prayer, on retreat in the desert, Jesus says "yes" to the best and truest in himself and the orders and systems of this world.

Praying as Jesus Prayed: Moving against the Cultural Current

In the 21st chapter of the Gospel of John, the newly resurrected Jesus appears to Peter and confronts him with the alternative direction their relationship would take Peter if he really did love and follow Jesus faithfully. There had been a large gap between Peter's rhetoric and his actions. Jesus asks Peter several times if he loves him, and each time Peter replies in the affirmative. Jesus also tells him to care for the friends and followers he is leaving behind. The last time Jesus asks Peter if he loves him, Peter replies in a somewhat exasperated and hurt tone, "Lord, you know everything, you know that I love you." Again Jesus tells him, "Feed my sheep," and then adds, "Very truly, I tell you, when you were younger, you used to fasten your own belt and go wherever you wished. But when you grow old, you will stretch out your hands, and someone else will fasten a belt around you and take you where you do not wish to go." (He said this to indicate the kind of death by which [Peter] would glorify God.) After this [Jesus] said to him, "Follow me" (John 21:16–19).

This story suggests that when we come before the One Who Is—in full loving attention through our embodied, holistic way of praying—we are, in essence, "stretching out our hands" in faith and consenting to allow Jesus to fasten his belt around us and lead us in a direction we might not go otherwise. This is what makes Jesus and his spirituality so threatening to the powers of this world. To follow Jesus in the twenty-first century will require a comprehensive, radically embodied way of praying that is substantial and deep enough to sustain us in conditions comparable to the one Jesus faced with Satan in the desert, and to what Peter and the other disciples faced in the first century. Jesus' "vine and branches" spirituality (John 15:1–8) will, in effect, be like him tying a belt around us and moving us counter to the culture, toward a compassionate, costly engagement with not only ourselves and each other, but also with the systems, structures, and powers of this world to the glory of God.

Taking Jesus Seriously:
"Dear Dr. Borg"

A few years ago Dr. Marcus Borg came to speak about his work on the historical Jesus at Virginia Theological Seminary in Alexandria, Virginia, from which I graduated in the mid-1970s. His lectures were entitled "Taking Jesus Seriously." This title drew me to the event but by the end of it I felt that just the opposite had happened—Jesus had not been taken seriously at all. If Jesus had been taken seriously, I reasoned, most everyone in that room would have been uncomfortable, threatened, and upset to some degree with Jesus, his radical gospel, and the social, political, and economic implications as outlined in Dr. Borg's talks.

The audience was primarily a middle- to upper-middle-class, white, well-educated group of people who would be considered the "Christian-haves" of our society and world. Yet there seemed to be no discomfort with Jesus and his alternative, which directly confronts and challenges such audiences and our position of power and privilege. There was little sense of the seriousness of Jesus' historical challenge to the status quo. To me, the intellectualizing, analyzing, arguing, and nitpicking around the historical Jesus seemed to have the effect of minimizing Jesus and inhibiting us from taking him and his call to comprehensive change seriously in any concrete way. So I wrote Dr. Borg and expressed these and other sentiments. In part I wrote:

> Over the years, I've seen a lot of people come to the inner city with high Christian idealism about serving the poor and following Jesus, only to see many of them leave burned out and disillusioned because their spiritual foundation was not deep, strong, and comprehensive enough. The harsh realities of life and ministry in this setting demand that the significance of the historical Jesus expand and grow in us rather than be diminished, because I believe the real, historical, risen Jesus is where authentic power, strength, and transformation ultimately abides.

In his reply Dr. Borg said:

> I share the passion I hear in your letter. I agree with you completely that the historical Jesus matters

greatly: it is who gives concrete, specific content to what it means to follow him (including dying to an old way of being, and becoming passionate about "the least of these"), which for me includes not only charity and deeds of compassion, but also a passion for social justice.

And I think (and say) that a Christian life which does not yet see the sociopolitical meaning of the gospels is one that is not yet fully mature. I think Jesus as I understand him invites us to become radically centered in God (what I mean by "spirituality"), passionate about compassion in the world (including passion for social justice).

Together, these two are the path of discipleship. Spirituality and politics go together and I see the union of the two in the most central figures of the biblical tradition: Moses, the prophets, and Jesus, to name the big ones. And I see the combination of these two as constituting the path of discipleship: dying to an old way of being, and being transformed into a new way of seeing, centering and acting. That new way of seeing will include a growing awareness of the role that domination systems play in inflicting unnecessary social misery upon so many. And I hope to lead my mainline audiences down the path of discipleship, or at least to give them a glimpse of what that path looks like.[14]

My prayer is that by God's grace, we who call ourselves Christians will commit ourselves to going down the path of a more fully matured, radically embodied, and Christ-centered spiritual practice that includes the political and social dimensions of the gospel. As we confront the issues that face us at the beginning of the twenty-first century, it will be essential.

Notes

1. Elizabeth O'Connor, *Journey Inward, Journey Outward* (New York: Harper and Row, 1968).

2. Hungry for a deeper spiritual life and weary with the destructive directions of their society, these men and women separated from mainstream society and went into the desert to develop a life of prayer and radical trust in God. One of the prayer disciplines they are reported to have developed was that of repeating a "prayer word" or phrase, often taken from the Bible, to help keep them more consciously centered in God throughout each moment of the day.

3. Walter Brueggemann, *Cadences of Home: Preaching Among Exiles* (Louisville, KY: Westminster John Knox Press, 1997), 1–14.

4. As quoted in Jürgen Moltmann, *God in Creation* (Minneapolis: Fortress Press, 1993), 244.

5. Thomas Ryan, CSP, *Prayer of Heart and Body: Meditation and Yoga as Christian Spiritual Practice* (New York: Paulist Press, 1995), 109, 111.

6. Thomas Ryan, CSP, *Wellness, Spirituality and Sports* (New York: Paulist Press, 1986), 35.

7. John Dunne as quoted in Basil Pennington, *Centering Prayer: Renewing an Ancient Christian Prayer Form* (New York: Doubleday, 1980), 129–30.

8. Karl Barth as quoted in Kenneth Leech, *True Prayer* (San Francisco: Harper and Row), 1968.

9. Henri J. M. Nouwen, *Out of Solitude: Three Meditations on the Christian Life* (Notre Dame, IN: Ave Maria Press, 1974), 13–14.

10. Goetz Kluge, "Trickle Down Trash, Squeeze Up Wealth," an article on global disparity on Kluge's Entropy and Inequality Measures website, http://poorcity.richcity.org, accessed April 29, 2003.

11. Arthur B. Kennickell, "Wealth Inequality Charts," excerpted on the United for a Fair Economy website, http://www.faireconomy.org/research/wealth_charts.html, accessed April 30, 2003.

12. Walter Wink, *Unmasking the Powers: The Invisible Forces That Determine Human Existence* (Philadelphia: Fortress Press, 1986), 18.

13. Ibid.

14. Correspondence, January 20, 1998, and November 13, 1998.

6.

Reclaiming the Body of Earth: Born Again of Water and Spirit

James Hall

At its root the Christian faith is an embodied faith, yet we have been alienated from our own bodies. But now we are recovering a faith that includes and celebrates the human body. What then of the rest of creation? Just as we have been alienated from our human bodies, so also we have been alienated from the earth around us. What does it mean to recover a faith that includes and celebrates not only the human body but also the earth's body?

Our present estrangement from the earth is poignantly illustrated by this story: A schoolteacher walking one day in the Botanical Gardens in New York City noticed two children, a boy of about six and his younger sister, chasing each other across the grass. As they raced downhill, the boy tripped over a root and fell forward, sprawling to the ground. He got up slowly, checking his elbows and knees for bruises. Suddenly a big smile spread across his face. "It's fun to fall on the grass," he said, astonished. "It's fun to fall on the grass." For the next ten minutes the little boy and his sister practiced falling—dashing across the grass and flinging themselves on it, laughing and giggling all the time. The school-teacher watched a long time, enchanted and appalled at this drama—clearly a new experience for these children.[1]

We are like those children; close encounters with nature are foreign to us. We have forgotten how to fall on grass. In that forgetting lies a significant diminishment of our human lives, body and soul, and a diminishment of earth as well. It is as if we moderns have "broken the everlasting covenant," and so "the earth dries up and withers" and "the inhabitants of earth dwindle" (Isa 24:4–6). We have forgotten who we are as image-bearers of the Creator and tenders of the land. We cannot fully know our own bodies until we know the body of the earth—the dust from which we were formed, the rock from which we were hewn, the grass beneath our feet.

Dust and Breath:
The Earth from Which We Came

The Lord God formed man from the dust of the ground, and breathed into his nostrils the breath of life; and the man became a living being. (Gen 2:7)

The biblical teaching about the relationship from the beginning between the human body and the earth could not be more explicit. This is especially true when one considers that the Hebrew word for man *(adam)* is closely related to the word for ground *(adamah)*—and is also the name *Adam* (Gen 2:20). To this dust of the earth God adds the breath of life. Our Christian tradition has often understood the "breath of life" as soul—that dimension of the human that sets the human apart from everything else in creation. A special divine element may indeed be breathed into the human by God, but the phrase "breath of life" *(neshamah)* has a broader meaning in Old Testament usage. Sometimes it is God's breath coming in power to grant or take away life, including that of the nonhuman (Gen 7:21–22, Job 37:10), and sometime it is man's breath, in a literal sense, the measure of his life (1 Kgs 17:17). The breath of life that God breathes into us is something that we share with all living creatures.

Our bodies, then—formed from the dust of earth and, like all living things, brought to life by the breath of God—share a deep intimacy with God and all other created things. This is the intimacy that the psalmist speaks of when he says, "You knit me together in my mother's womb....My frame was not hidden from you when I was being made in secret, intricately woven in the depths of the earth" (Ps 139:13, 15).

The intuitive wisdom of the biblical narrative is confirmed by what we have learned from the sciences of cosmology, ecology, and human evolution. In our study of the universe we have discovered that all things have a common origin and a common fifteen-billion-year story. The dust of the earth from which we were made comes from the dust of early stars whose supernova explosions gave rise to the heavier elements needed for life to emerge.[2] The view from space of our blue-green earth home gives us a deep appreciation of how small and fragile, yet infinitely special, is our place in the universe. From ecology we learn that we are an integral part of highly interrelated and inter-dependent planetary systems; we are dependent on their proper function for our ongoing breath of life.

We humans became who we are as a species on this planet over tens of thousands of years of being in intimate contact with creation around us. Our children grew up with their hands in the clay earth; their ears filled with the sounds of wind and storm and the gentle rustle of leaves on the trees; their eyes filled with the wonder of clouds crossing the sky, of ants at play. In the mysterious and beautiful world around them, they found clues to the meaning of life embodied in natural things; everyday life was filled with spiritual significance and encounter. Only recently have we lost contact with the earth out of which we were made, and on which we depend for life and sanity. Some think that this is why we are blindly destroying our habitat.[3] In our alienation from the earth, have we gone mad?

We live in a time of great devastation of both natural and human life on the planet. Pope John Paul II says that we are living in a culture of death, and he extends the defense of life to include all creation.[4] Others say that we are living in the adolescence of our species and need to grow up.[5] The naturalist Stephanie Mills, reflecting on the loss of frogs and the prospect of "spring going mute," writes, "Our species is now in a position akin to that of the drunk driver who kills a family in a hit-and-run accident, and then has to take sober responsibility for the slaughter."[6] I wonder, we human ones, especially in the West, are we the drunk drivers whose crash kills a family? Is our insanity simply the normal psychopathology of adolescence? Are we not yet fully mature sons and daughters of God—teenagers not fully mature in Christ—just crazy kids? All creation cries out, "Grow up! Grow up, or we will all be killed in your automobile accident."

We were formed of the dust of the earth; God breathed into our nostrils the breath of life. As a species we grew up in intimate relation with the natural world around us. Now we have become lost. Like the Prodigal of which Jesus spoke, we have left home, squandered our inheritance in self-centered living, and need to come to our senses. Our urgent task is to rediscover our place in the created order, to return home.

A Living Universe:
The Work of God's Hands

Ever since the creation of the world, God's eternal power and divine nature, invisible though they are, have been understood and seen through the things he has made. (Rom 1:20)

As we become aware that our bodies are intimately related to the earth's body, we may wonder, How does this relate to our faith? From the perspective of the Christian faith, so deeply incarnational, so much an embodied faith, we must ask, How is God embodied in the earth around us?

Again, the biblical teaching is clear: creation is fundamental to our understanding of who God is. All creation—the things that God has made—reveals to us the divinity of God, fills us with awe and wonder, and draws us to God. The craft leads us to, and informs us about, the maker of the craft. Thomas Berry poses the question, "What would our sense of the divine be if we lived on the moon?" He responds that if we lived on the moon, our sense of the divine would reflect the lunar landscape—it would not be anything like what we have at present.[7] Without the mountains reaching to the sky, without the shapes and colors of the flowers, without the music of the birds, how will we see "God's eternal power and divine nature through the things he has made?"

The psalms are full of images of God made visible in creation: "The heavens are telling the glory of God…." (Ps 19). "You make the winds your messengers, fire and flame your ministers" (Ps 104:4). A divine word is spoken, without language, in all the earth. The second half of Psalm 19 speaks of a written word (the law), another form of God's revelation. Subsequently early Christian saints spoke of the two books of God's revelation—the Bible and the book of creation. One of the desert fathers, Saint Anthony, when asked how he could live a devout life in the desert far from access to holy books, said, "My book is the nature of created things; whenever I want to read the word of God, it is there before me."[8] Over the centuries the mystical tradition in the Church has carried this wisdom. Meister Eckhart wrote, "Apprehend God in all things, for God is in all things. Every single creature is full of God, and is a book about God. Every creature is a word of God."[9]

The wisdom tradition in the Bible teaches that divine wisdom is embedded and embodied in creation. In Job we read:

"But ask the animals and they will teach you;
the birds of the air, and they will tell you;

> ask the plants of the earth and they will teach you;
>   and the fish of the sea will declare to you.
> Who among all these does not know
>   that the hand of the LORD has done this?
> In [God's] hand is the life of every living thing
>   and the breath of every human being."
>
> (Job 12:7–10)

Wisdom laid the earth's foundations (Prov 3:19), and by availing ourselves of that wisdom embedded in earth, we prosper. The writer of the Wisdom of Solomon acknowledges God as the source of understanding "the structure of the world and the activity of the elements…the natures of animals and the tempers of wild animals…the powers of winds and the thoughts of human beings…the variety of plants and the virtues of roots" (Wis 7:17, 20). This is wisdom that "…pervades and permeates all things; like a fine mist she rises from the power of God" (7:24–25; Rev. English Bible).

It is in the gospel stories of Jesus that we recognize how present and intimately available God is in creation. The story begins with Jesus' birth in a manger—a place where animals were kept, most likely a cave in the hillside. God's incarnation in human form begins in the earth itself. Years later, Jesus responds to the cry of John the Baptist, "In the wilderness prepare the way of the Lord." Then and now, John and his cry embody the undomesticated wildness of God. In that remote setting, Jesus was baptized, and as he came up out of the water a voice from heaven declared, "You are my beloved." The voice would speak this word yet once more—this time on a remote mountaintop (the Mount of Transfiguration). Throughout his ministry Jesus withdrew to remote mountain and desert places to pray. On the night before he was arrested, he went to a quiet garden to pour out his anguish and grief. For Jesus the most intimate moments with God took place in the desert, on the mountain, in the garden, among the wildness and beauty of God's creation.

To speak of the earth or creation as the embodiment of God is very different from saying that the earth is God. The beauty and majesty of God revealed in the natural world around us may be essential for our understanding of God, but the created things themselves do not then become god or gods. The writer of the book of the Wisdom of Solomon bemoans the fools who, though they observed his handiwork, failed to recognize the maker of the craft and thought that "fire, or wind, or swift air, or the circle of the stars, or turbulent water, or the luminaries of heaven were the gods that rule the world" (Wis 13:1–2). In the desert for forty days Jesus was among the wild beasts, and angels attended to him. In a storm at sea, he even spoke to the winds and waves. Despite this deep engagement with creation, no one would think that for Jesus nature was god or would accuse him of earth worship.

In following Jesus, in living this embodied faith, we are invited to return to the wild, beautiful, and God-breathed landscapes of this, our earth home. We are invited, like Moses, to awaken to the fire blazing out from a bush, to turn aside to see it, and to recognize that we are standing on holy ground.

Earth Made Whole:
The Work of Christ

He has made known to us the mystery of his will, according to his good pleasure that he set forth in Christ, as a plan for the fullness of time, to gather up all things in him, things in heaven and things on earth. (Eph 1:9–10)

We live in a sacred universe filled with the presence of God by whose hands it was, and is ever being, formed and shaped, our bodies intimately embedded therein. From the perspective of the Christian faith, then, we must ask, where in this sacred universe is Christ embodied? We know that he is present in the visible Church, which we call the Body of Christ. We know that he is present in the Eucharist. Further, we know that he is also present, and in some sense embodied, in ongoing creative/redemptive work. Christ is at work making the world whole.

We often think of the present redemptive work of Christ in solely human terms, although in the letters of Paul, Christ's redemptive work is extended to all the created order, including the human. In anticipation of the glory ahead, Paul says that, "The creation waits with eager longing…has been groaning in labor pains until now" (Rom 8:19, 22). All things, whether on earth or in heaven, Paul says, hold together in Jesus and will be reconciled through him (Col 1:17, 20); all things in heaven and on earth will be gathered up in Christ (Eph 1:10).

In exploring this understanding of the risen Christ—often referred to as the cosmic Christ—Robert Faricy, SJ, concludes that, "First, Christ is the head of the Church and the Church is his body; secondly, Christ is the head of the cosmos, and the cosmos is his body." As Faricy sees it, since in Christ the whole fullness of the deity dwells bodily (Col 2:9), the cosmos may be viewed as the Body of Christ.[10] The embodiment of Christ in the world of matter was central to another Jesuit, Pierre Teilhard de Chardin, who spoke of "how the universe, in all its power and multiplicity, came to assume for me the lineaments of the face of Christ."[11]

The mystical and contemplative tradition in the Church has always recognized a strong connection between the risen Christ and the natural world. Nature is a metaphor for the humanity of Christ in Jesus' own teaching ("I am the true vine"—John 15:1) and for Saint John of the Cross, Jesus is "…the mountains, the lonely wooded valleys, the strange islands, the noisy rivers, the whistling of winds in love."[12] The contemporary importance of this understanding is underscored by Father Richard Rohr, the founder of the Center for Action and Contemplation. In speaking about rebuilding the Church, Rohr said, "If you're not interested in the plant world, the animal world, the physical world, you haven't discovered the great Christ yet; your Christ is too small."[13]

Even as we look to the cosmic Christ to redeem all things, we are all too aware that much remains to be redeemed. God suffers at the hands of a godless world;[14] Christ suffers in the pain of creation, and suffers it bodily if we accept the cosmos as Christ's body. Such a view is entirely consistent with the life of Jesus of

Nazareth, whose ministry was so bodily focused—in feeding the body, in healing the body, and whose dying body bore such grievous pain. In fact Jesus' solidarity with the suffering and oppressed implies that Christ today also suffers in solidarity with the oppressed, including the oppressed nonhuman and the earth itself.[15] The cosmic Christ, then, is embodied in the world in solidarity with, and working to redeem, the suffering and oppressed, including both the human and the nonhuman, "things in heaven and things on earth" (Eph 1:9).

Take Off Your Shoes:
An Embodied Prayer with the Earth

Remove the sandals from your feet, for the place on which you are standing is holy ground. (Exod 3:5)

Prayer is nothing but the inhaling and exhaling of the one breath of the universe. (Hildegard of Bingen)

The earth that shares dust and breath of life with us, the earth that is God's handiwork, a direct revelation of God to us, the earth where Christ suffers and works for redemption—this earth invites us to pray. We are invited to a prayer of embodiment that includes all created things. We know that in our present alienation from our bodies, from other humans, and from the community of life on earth, the prayer of embodiment extended to include the earth is an essential spiritual practice if life—including human life—is going to flourish on this planet.

How do we learn to pray the prayer of embodiment with all creation? One way we can begin is by going to a less inhabited, natural place. We know that Jesus, like the prophets before and the saints since, often went away to a "desert" place to pray. For us, that desert place may be a quiet garden, a bit of nearby parkland, or sometimes even a true desert or wilderness area. Such a place, if it is accessible and we go there often, will become a special and sacred place where we can meet God in the things he has made.

As we come to our special place, we can begin our prayer by quieting our minds, being aware of our bodies and our breath, and attending to our senses. When we are ready, we can begin to explore the world we have just entered. In doing this we will need to rediscover a childlike sense of wonder—remembering the words of Rachel Carson: "A child's world is fresh and new and beautiful, full of wonder and excitement....If I had influence with the good fairy who is supposed to preside over the christening of all children, I should ask that her gift to each child in the world would be a sense of wonder so indestructible that it would last throughout life, as an unfailing antidote against the boredom and disenchantments of later years, the sterile preoccupation with things artificial, the alienation from the source of our strength."[16] Could this sense of wonder be part of what Jesus was talking about when he said that in order to enter the Kingdom of God we must receive it as a little child? (Luke 18:17).

We begin with wonder, but in time we will want to know more about the butterflies, the trees, the rocks that are part of our special place. As with the written scripture, there are books to help us understand the lost scripture of the earth. We need the help of scripture scholars, scholars of the scripture of the earth. Most of us do not know much about the plant world, the animal world, the physical world where we live. We are aliens in our native land!

Jon Young, founder of the Kamana School of Wilderness Awareness Studies, tells a story from his earlier days of teaching school. He asked his class to imagine that they were on a trip to the Kalahari in Africa and a Bushman was taking them through the land he lived in. The Bushman would point to an animal track and ask what animal made this, what was its mood, which way was it going, and when was it here. The class would say they didn't know. Then the Bushman would point out a plant and ask what it was used for and how it could help us now, and the class wouldn't know. The Bushman would ask which way was north, and what about that birdsong—what was going on, what was the bird saying, and the class wouldn't know. When Jon asked the class why they wouldn't know, they replied by saying, how could they know, they were just tourists. Then Jon gave them a quiz with photographs and questions about their own nearby parks and backyards, and still they didn't know the answers.[17] Surely they (and we then), are just "tourists," aliens, even in our own land.

The beginning practice of prayer of embodiment extended to the earth is very nourishing and can be very healing. As we recover our childlike sense of wonder and curiosity about the natural world, as we learn its secrets and appreciate its beauty, our own creativity is rekindled. We respond to the wonders of God's creation with gestures and movements, song and dance, poetry and art. Creation has always been the source of our creativity. Without rivers how could there be poems? Without forests, deserts, mountains, prairies, what will awaken the seed of divine imagination planted within us? We receive a great blessing as we step away from the man-made world and into the world that God made. Our prayer is full of gratitude.

As we engage in this form of prayer—in communion with God and with Christ in the natural world, and in touch with the wisdom of the book of creation—there is no need to abandon the Bible. To the contrary, when we lay the written scripture, so full of images from the natural world, beside the scripture of the earth, our understanding of each is enhanced. There is a story from the life of the Celtic saints that beautifully illustrates the marriage of written and earth scripture. One snowy night Saint Kevin of Glendalough went into the lake up to his waist, as was his practice, to recite the divine office. As he was reading his psalms, the psalter fell into the lake and sank to some depth. An angel came to reassure him that it was not lost. Soon an otter came up from the depths of the lake, the book in his mouth, and gave it to Kevin. Not a single letter was blotched.[18]

We cannot be in our special place, in hardly any natural place on this planet today, however, without also hearing a deep cry of anguish. The stars are not as bright as they once were; there are fewer bluebirds and monarch butterflies; the voices of the spring peepers grow weaker by the year. In our foray back into the natural world we encounter not only the incarnation

(God's eternal power and divine nature made visible), but also the crucifixion—God's suffering at the hands of a godless world.[19] We find ourselves in a garden of tears, our path of beauty having become the Way of the Cross.

For anyone who has followed Jesus for very long, this cannot be a surprise. The beauty of a newborn child is a wonder to behold, but who can begin to take in the suffering of children on this planet today? And the tears of our children are the water in our creeks and rivers and oceans; it is all one creation, beautiful and broken. Yet the story does not end with crucifixion—not the story of Christ, not the story of the universe. God always will have the last word; Christ will reconcile all things in heaven and on earth.

Stories of Recovery and Rebirth

It is wonderful to pray, as Jesus did, in a place of natural beauty—a quiet garden or a hillside with a view. There is, however, a subtle but important distinction between nature as backdrop for prayer, on the one hand, and creation as communion with the presence of God, which is the prayer itself, on the other. The latter is the essence of what the prayer of embodiment that includes the earth is about. Present in our bodies, we are aware of the presence of God and of Christ in the earth's body around us. Let me share with you what this looks like through three stories. The first two relate to experiences in the lives of members of my church and family, and the last concerns changes in the water that runs through the property of our church retreat center.

Wind of God

...a wind [spirit, ruach] from God swept over the face of the waters. (Gen 1:2)

Ahead on the nearly empty highway, the lone sign read, "South Dakota." Our three day trip from "the East" was almost over. I pulled off the road; one of the kids in our church youth group wanted a photo of the sign to record this moment in our trip. Stepping out of the car my face recorded a brisk westerly wind, a wind that would not quit for the whole of our stay. My eyes registered a few slight undulations in the otherwise straight horizon, too many miles away to calculate. There is nothing here, I thought. Nothing but immense sky, waving grass, and the wind.

We soon arrived at our destination, a mission school on the Rosebud Reservation. Father Noah Brokenleg greeted us. We were full of questions: "What should we call you, Father Brokenleg?" "What time should we be up in the morning?" "What kind of work project do you have for us?" "When do we start?" Father Brokenleg just smiled. After a moment he said, "You're out here to relax; you people always come out here with your programs and schedules—at such and such a time we will do this, and so forth. Just relax and take time to get a feeling for how we live out here."

RECLAIMING THE BODY OF EARTH

We had no choice but to adopt Father Brokenleg's approach. A day passed, two days passed; still there was no work. We relaxed. We slowed down. When we were ready to listen, Father Brokenleg said, "Here's what you do while you're out here. Find your small but important place in creation, and learn to find beauty in the commonplace."

Who can know what this experience will mean in the lives of these young people? One of them reflected afterward that it was easy to find the beauty around us—from the "tiniest stalk of grass to the great plains sky." Her experience of both the beauty and the human distress on the reservation gave birth to questions about God and God's creation. Yet God's revelation in nature is more than questions and answers; it is encounter with divine presence. What we know of God's presence in nature we perceive with our hearts and bodies, perhaps more than with our minds. The young people in the work camp in South Dakota could tell you what the spirituality of embodiment feels like. They experienced the land as revelatory of God—the abstract became real as they hiked through the tall grass toward hills that refused to draw closer, and returned with dusty feet, windblown hair, and eyes wide open. Their faces shone as if they had been in the presence of God. And surely they had, for they had experienced God in wind and earth, sun and sky.

The Rock from Which You Were Hewn

Look to the rock from which you were hewn. (Isa 51:1)

"The coastal hiking trail south of Oiseau Bay is rugged, poorly marked, and easily confused with game trails." So reads this warning in the brochure for Pukaskwa National Park, a wilderness park along the Canadian coast of Lake Superior—the "wild shore of an inland sea." A three-hour ride on an old tugboat past fir-lined islands and deep coves brought us to the mouth of the North Swallow River, the south end of the coastal hiking trail. The challenge before us was to hike back.

I awoke at 3 a.m. the night before our first day on the trail. The sound of wind flapping the tent fly and the echoes of thunder out on the lake brought me scurrying outside to add ropes from tent to tree and tree to tent. At daybreak I peered outside. I could not be certain if the rain had stopped; water dripped from trees, filled the air. I had not slept well.

On this day it seemed impossible to hike for miles with full packs over wet, rocky hills and headlands. We began with the possible—bringing water from the lake, lighting the stove. With sips of hot coffee and spoonfuls of oatmeal steaming from the bowl, we decided to pack up. As I folded the wet tent into its stuff sack, I wondered how much extra weight of water I was obliged to carry. I recalled once laughing at a suggestion to trim off my toothbrush handle to save weight. I did not laugh that morning. We headed out, our son, Jon, the trail finder in the lead. We paused to voice a simple prayer for safety and protection. At the first small rise a fresh gust of wind blew light rain in our faces.

RECLAIMING THE BODY OF EARTH

The rock on which we walked is the Canadian Shield, extruded onto the surface of the planet over two billion years ago, as life was just beginning. It bore the marks of much weathering, of eras warmer and colder, of glaciers come and gone. On this day I came to know this rock more intimately than I had ever known rock before. I avoided the smooth surfaces, slippery as the ice that shaped them. My eyes traced the cracks and rough quartz veins where my foot could hold. I tested blue-green lichen, black lichen, and soft moss—the latter certain to make me slip. I saw the winding roots of trees clasping at rock and crevice, speaking of lifetimes of resistance to the weight of storms. My prayer life deepened as I moved from metaphor to moment; prayer was every step.

At 4 p.m. we arrived at the mouth of the White Spruce River. Jon, having tried trails true and false, had fallen three times, but was OK. Our feet sank pleasantly into soft sand on the shore of a little cove; our steps slowed as we gazed out into dense fog, searching in vain for hints of blue water or fir-lined island. We joined hands, giving thanks for a safe journey. I unrolled the wet tent, clip-locked it to the poles, and unpacked the stove, pot, cups, bowls, spoons, and the makings of dinner. The fog lifted at sunset; two loons fished between the cove and the open lake. Jon made a driftwood fire on the narrow sand beach. My heart filled with a chorus from the psalms, its meaning deepened by the experience of the day past:

> The LORD is my rock, my fortress, and my deliverer,
> my God, my rock in whom I take refuge....

JAMES HALL

The LORD lives! Blessed be my rock,
and exalted be the God of my salvation.

(Ps 18:2, 46)

Spring of Living Water

...but those who drink of the water that I will give them
will never be thirsty. The water that I will give will
become in them a spring of water gushing up to eternal
life. (John 4:14)

In the wooded valley behind the Lodge of the Carpenter at Dayspring—our church retreat center in the Maryland suburbs of Washington, DC—there is a small creek. A little path follows the creek upstream, here skirting a fallen chestnut oak, there winding through a grove of mountain laurel. The creek has long ago made its own path, splashing over rock ledges, dancing with rays of filtered sun, voicing its song in the dark wood.

In years past we would follow this creek upstream, beyond where the path gave out, to its source in one of several small springs at the low end of an old pasture. Here, hidden within clumps of tall green reeds and rushes, water bubbled forth out of the ground. On hot days we would dip our hands in the clear water and cool our faces. It was as if we had entered another world, lost ourselves in a sacred kingdom, tasted living water.

One late winter day, walking upstream to the spring, we first noticed signs of the change that was to come—numbered stakes with orange plastic tape on them, ax marks on trees. We heard that 450 houses were to be built in this old pasture. On retreat, a few days before Easter, I walked upstream to visit the spring. Where the water had bubbled forth from clumps of reeds and rushes, a large storm-water sediment basin had been freshly dug in the orange-brown clay soil. "What happened to the spring?" I cried. Looking closely at the uphill wall of the nearly empty basin, about two feet from the top, I saw a small trickle of water emerging from the wall and running down into the basin. I wrote in my journal:

> Like a deep longing my stream you refuse to lose my
>   attention;
> for me it was you bled and did not die, bleeding even
>   now;
> stream longing, Christ longing in me,
> carry me on your sparkling waters all the way home.

On Good Friday we gathered next to a wild rosebush on some remaining meadow grass near the sediment basin. We placed by the bush a photograph of the spring, a small hand-hewn wooden cross, and a candle, and we prayed.

Years have passed, and now most of the 450 houses have been built. The water quality in the creek, which we monitor by sampling the insect life in the streambed, has greatly declined. One spring, during the Easter season, after another disappointing sample from our monitoring site, we walked down the stream valley to where house-sized boulders lie beside the stream. Here, opposite the boulders, a small tributary joins the main stream. The tributary is small enough to step across with ease, the water running transparent over its cobbled bed. We took a sample, just a small one, to check the water quality. The sample was alive with a diversity of organisms, some found only in the highest quality streams in the county. We marveled at how this little tributary could be so pure, so full of life.

Where did this water come from? We followed the tributary upstream until it disappeared in a dense thicket in an old abandoned farm field, now county parkland. The old field is returning to forest, its natural state, but not without a struggle. Invasive, non-native honeysuckle vines and multiflora rose girdle the young trees; tent caterpillars feast on the first crop of cherry leaves; the deer rub their antlers on the bark of young cherry and red cedar, often killing them. But here a forest is going to return. We spotted a cherry tree that, against all odds, is thirty feet tall. A red cedar, rubbed hard by a deer, lay broken in half, brown and dry on the ground. Looking closer we saw emerging from the base of the broken stump dense sprouts of new growth.

We walked back down the tributary into the deep shade of the stream valley and climbed up on the huge boulders. Below us the clear water of the small tributary entered the slightly turbid water of the main stream and was lost. But everything within me cried out that it was not lost! True, some things have died and are lost forever, but beneath the suffering and death, the deep undercurrent of God's infinite creativity and redeeming mercy endures. To know Christ and the power of his resurrection is to be a little tributary of faith, a spring of living water, pouring itself into the mainstream of this world.

Born Again of Water and Spirit

Very truly I tell you, no one can enter the kingdom of God without being born of water and Spirit. (John 3:5)

Wind of God, rock from which we were hewn, spring of living water—all these invite us to an experience of embodied prayer. Like the children in the Botanical Garden in New York City, we are drawn to fling ourselves on the grass and discover that it is fun to fall on grass. For those who have lost that intimate communion with God in creation, the experience will be like a rebirth.

When Nicodemus, the Jewish Pharisee, comes to Jesus at night, Jesus tells him he must be born again. Nicodemus wonders how someone can be born when he is old. "Can one enter a second time into the mother's womb and be born"? he asks. Jesus replies that it is about being born of water and spirit, but the mystery lingers. Perhaps Jesus was referring to the future sacrament of baptism and the baptism of the Holy Spirit. But is that all Jesus meant? What if Jesus intended the mystery to linger? In the beginning of creation, "*ruach* (spirit or wind) of God swept over the face of the waters" (Gen 1:2). What if it still does, waiting to give birth?

Our recovery of the body of the earth, our being born again of water and spirit, is essential if life is to survive and flourish on our planet. Our return to earth in the prayer of embodiment is just as essential if our faith journey is going to flourish. Here before us, under our feet, is the world where God reigns. As he spoke to Moses, so God speaks to us today from the bush of fire: Take off your shoes, you are standing on holy ground.

Notes

1. Christian McEwen, "Inside a Stone," *Orion Afield* 2, no 2 (1998): 32.

2. Brian Swimme and Thomas Berry, CP, *The Universe Story* (San Francisco: Harper, 1992), 48–49.

3. Paul Shepard, *Nature and Madness* (San Francisco: Sierra Club Books, 1982), 6–15.

4. Quoted in *At Home in the Web of Life: A Pastoral Message on Sustainable Communities in Appalachia*, the Catholic Bishops of Appalachia (Webster Springs, WV: Catholic Committee of Appalachia, 1995), 4; originally from Pope John Paul II, *Evangelium Vitae* (1995, Sections 12, 22) and *The Ecological Crisis: A Common Responsibility* (Washington, DC: US Catholic Conference, 1991).

5. Thomas Berry, *The Dream of the Earth* (San Francisco: Sierra Club Books, 1988), 47–49.

6. Stephanie Mills, *Epicurean Simplicity* (Washington, DC: Island Press, 2002), 72.

7. Thomas Berry, CP, *Befriending the Earth: A Theology of Reconciliation Between Humans and the Earth* (Mystic, CT: Twenty-Third Publications, 1991), 9.

8. Quoted in Belden Lane, *The Solace of Fierce Landscapes: Exploring Desert and Mountain Spirituality* (New York: Oxford University Press, 1998), 165; originally from *Evagrius Ponticus, Capita Practica ad Anatolium*, 92 in PG:40.1249B.

9. Quoted in *Earth Prayers*, ed. Elizabeth Roberts and Elias Amidon (San Francisco: Harpers, 1991), 251, originally from *Meditations*

with Meister Eckhart by Matthew Fox (Santa Fe, NM: Bear & Company Inc, 1983).

10. Robert Faricy, *Wind and Sea Obey Him: Approaches to a Theology of Nature* (Westminster, MD: Christian Classics, Inc., 1988), 10.

11. Pierre Teilhard de Chardin, *Hymn of the Universe,* quoted in Ursula King, *Pierre Teilhard de Chardin: Writings* (New York: Orbis Books, 1999), 103.

12. Faricy, 72–73. The quote from St. John of the Cross is from his *Cancionnes entre el alma y el Esposo* (Third Song of the Bride).

13. Richard Rohr, *Rebuild the Church,* Audiotape A628 (Cincinnati, OH: St. Anthony Messenger Press, 1994).

14. The phrase is from Dietrich Bonhoeffer, *Letters and Papers from Prison,* ed. Eberhard Bethge (New York: Macmillan, 1953), 361.

15. Sallie McFague, *The Body of God: An Ecological Theology* (Minneapolis, MN: Fortress Press, 1993), 164.

16. Rachel Carson, *The Sense of Wonder* (Covelo, CA: The Nature Company, n.d.; originally published by Harper and Row, New York, 1956).

17. Jon Young, *Seeing through Native Eyes: Understanding the Language of Nature,* audiotape (La Honda, CA: Owlink Media, USA, 1996).

18. Edward Sellner, *Wisdom of the Celtic Saints* (Notre Dame, IN: Ave Maria Press, 1993), 160.

19. Rohr, *Rebuild the Church.*

Contributors

Jim Dickerson is a native of Arkansas and resident of inner-city Washington, DC, where he and his wife Grace have lived, worked, and raised their three children over the past thirty-one years. He is founder and Chair of Manna, Inc., a nationally recognized, non-profit, affordable-housing and community-development organization. He is also pastor of New Community Church—a small, highly active, neighborhood-based church affiliated with Church of the Saviour.

James Hall practiced family medicine for twenty-two years at an inner-city health clinic associated with the Church of the Savior in Washington, DC; he also had an academic appointment at a teaching hospital affiliated with George Washington University Medical School. He is currently studying natural history and ecology and building a new earth-ministry center at Dayspring, the church's retreat farm. He and his wife lead retreats and teach classes on rediscovering the earth as teacher and healer, on living simply, and on finding new food for the soul.

Casey Rock attended the University of Toronto where she completed her Bachelor of Arts and Master of Library Science degrees. She worked as a librarian and researcher for the Canadian Broadcast Corporation while raising three children. More recently she received a Master of Divinity degree from the

CONTRIBUTORS

University of St. Michael's College, and yoga teacher certification from the Kripalu Center. She currently resides with her husband in Toronto where she teaches and writes.

Thomas Ryan, CSP, is a member of the Paulist Fathers community and directs the Paulist North American Office for Ecumenical and Interfaith Relations in New York City. Among his nine books are *Disciplines for Christian Living, Prayer of Heart and Body,* and *Four Steps to Spiritual Freedom* (Paulist Press). A long-abiding passion for spirituality has permeated his ministerial life working for Christian unity and interfaith understanding. He leads ecumenical retreats and congregational renewal events entitled Gospel Call.

James A. Wiseman, OSB, is a Benedictine monk of St. Anselm's Abbey in Washington, DC, and an associate professor of theology at The Catholic University of America, where he served for five years as chair of the theology department. His most recent book is *Theology and Modern Science* (Continuum, 2002). He is also the co-editor of *Light from Light: An Anthology of Christian Mysticism* (Paulist Press, 2001) and the translator of four treatises of the Flemish mystic John Ruusbroec for the Paulist Press series The Classics of Western Spirituality.